1,423 QI FACTS

John Lloyd CBE is the creator of QI and founding producer of *The News Quiz, Not the Nine O'Clock News, Spitting Image, Blackadder* and *No Such Thing As The News*. His favourite page is 252.

James Harkin, QI's Head Elf, presents the QI Elves' podcast *No Such Thing As A Fish* and BBC2's *No Such Thing As The News*. He also produces BBC Radio 4's *The Museum of Curiosity*. His favourite page is 21.

Anne Miller is a scriptwriter and researcher for QI. She is Head Researcher for *The Museum of Curiosity*. Her favourite page is 304.

A QUITE INTERESTING BOOK

1,423 QI FACTS

TO BOWL YOU OVER

Compiled by
John Lloyd, James Harkin
& Anne Miller

FABER & FABER

First published in 2017
by Faber & Faber Ltd
Bloomsbury House
74–77 Great Russell Street
London WC1B 3DA

Typeset by Ian Bahrami
Printed and bound in England by CPI Group (UK) Ltd,
Croydon CR0 4YY

A CIP record for this book
is available from the British Library

ISBN 978–0–571–33910–5

2 4 6 8 10 9 7 5 3 1

Contents

Operating Instructions

This new collection of *1,423 QI Facts* may *look* like a book, but it's actually a portal.

Though you can read the whole thing in a couple of hours, each little nugget is just the visible tip of an information iceberg.

So, if you doubt any of the facts, or would like to know more, go online to:

qi.com/1423

In the search box, enter the *page number* of the fact that interests you. This will reveal our main source for each fact on the page, as shown overleaf.

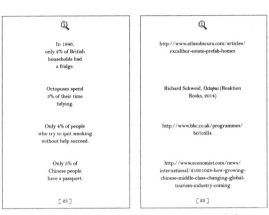

In 1946,
only 2% of British
households had
a fridge.

Octopuses spend
3% of their time
tidying.

Only 4% of people
who try to quit smoking
without help succeed.

Only 5% of
Chinese people
have a passport.

[25]

http://www.atlasobscura.com/articles/
excalibur-estate-prefab-homes

Richard Schweid, *Octopus* (Reaktion
Books, 2014)

http://www.bbc.co.uk/programmes/
b07c6ll4

http://www.economist.com/news/
international/21601028-how-growing-
chinese-middle-class-changing-global-
tourism-industry-coming

[25]

Page in book   *Page in source finder*

Click on any link to get the full explanation and all the background details.

To our surprise, we've found this feature is of particular value to teachers, who can start each lesson with a QI fact related to what they have to say. When asked 'Why?', the teacher (having read the source material) can confidently say: 'I'll tell you exactly why . . .'

But you don't need to be a teacher to do this – you can educate yourself. It's what the three of us have been doing every working day these last few years.

We hope you'll be as bowled over as we were.

JOHN LLOYD, JAMES HARKIN
& ANNE MILLER

*There is quite a good deal
of information in the book.
I regret this very much.*

MARK TWAIN

(1835–1910)

1,423 is
the Guinness World Record
for the largest number of authors
at a simultaneous
book signing.

1 in 4
Americans didn't
read a book
last year.

A book by
George H. W. Bush's dog
spent 23 weeks on the
US bestseller list.

Theresa May
owns more than 100
cookbooks.

Q1

John Bercow MP,
Speaker of the House of Commons,
has a cat called
Order.

There are
125,000 stray cats
in Istanbul.

The average
Australian cat
eats more fish per year
than the average
Australian.

Cuttlefish
have three hearts.

The North American
mosquito fish can
count up to four.

Fish can see
70 times further in air
than in water.

Golden-winged warblers
can detect tornadoes from
560 miles away.

35 tornadoes
are reported in
Britain each year.

In 1973,
the entire Internet
consisted of only
43 computers.

iPhones
in Venezuela cost
the equivalent of
£80,000 each.

Indonesia
has a volcano
that emits blue flames.

Iceland
has more volcanoes
than footballers.

More than half
of the Earth's surface
is not subject to any nation's laws.

It is illegal
to sell Stilton cheese
made in the village
of Stilton.

In northern Italy,
cheese is acceptable
as security on a
bank loan.

An Italian estate agent
was the inspiration for the
handsome, sadistic hero
of *Fifty Shades of Grey.*

The film of
Fifty Shades of Grey
was banned in Cambodia
because it depicted
'insane romance'.

North Korea banned
the disaster movie *2012*
in case it jinxed the
year 2012.

In French,
Jaws became
'The Teeth of the Sea'.

The spiders used in
Spider-Man and *Arachnophobia*
were social huntsman spiders
and completely harmless.

Spiders tune
their webs like
guitars.

Every year,
spiders consume
more food than whales.

Ogre-faced spiders
attract prey with their
excrement.

In 2017,
Australian scientists
discovered 50 new species
of spider in one 10-day
research trip.

10% of spiders
are missing at least one
of their legs.

In India,
termites' jaws
were once used to
close wounds.

In Brazil,
fish skin is used
to bandage burns.

The NHS
costs the UK
more than £116 billion
a year.

The British
eat more onions than
the French.

Ancient Egyptian priests were
not allowed to eat onions
in case it boosted
their libido.

The average person
has sex 5,778 times
in a lifetime.

Nicknames for
19th-century sex positions
included The Ordinary, The Spiky Chair
and The View of the Low Countries.

A sex manual
in Qing dynasty China
outlined 48 different ways to
fondle a mutilated foot.

Musical theatre
is the genre of music
least likely to be played
in the bedroom.

In 1917,
P. G. Wodehouse had
five musicals on Broadway
at the same time.

Ostentation funk
is a Brazilian musical genre
that celebrates the
middle-class
lifestyle.

40% of
working Britons
have less than £100
in savings.

1.7 million
Britons haven't got
a bank account.

The chief economist
at the Bank of England
has never owned a
credit card.

The Pope
doesn't know
how to use a computer.

Westminster Abbey
has a cleric called
Canon Ball.

The head of the
UK police task force
on knife crime is called
Alfred Hitchcock.

The man who holds
the British record for
summiting Everest
is a Mr K. Cool.

IKEA sofas
have Swedish names,
its rugs have Danish names
and its beds have Norwegian names.

Norwegian passports
display the aurora borealis
under a UV light.

You can be blocked
from getting a Swiss passport
if your neighbours find you
too annoying.

Horses
competing in
the Olympics have
their own passports and
fly business class.

A beer tap
on an aeroplane
would dispense
only foam.

The world's most popular beer
is called Snow and is
virtually unknown
outside China.

The most common job
in the UK is
'manager'.

In 2016,
a London company
advertised for an
'emoji translator'.

In 2017,
the US Secret Service
advertised for a 'social media
sarcasm spotter'.

If you blend
25 random pictures
from the Internet,
the result will
be orange.

'International orange'
is the specific shade of orange
used for NASA spacesuits,
the Tokyo Tower and the
Golden Gate Bridge.

Saturn's
North Pole is
blue.

NASA provided the
first American woman in space
with a specially designed
make-up kit.

American astronauts
on the International Space Station
can vote in elections
by email.

In 2015,
President Obama made it legal
for Americans to
own asteroids.

The smallest satellite
ever made weighs less than
a smartphone.

NASA
spacesuits are called
Extravehicular Mobility Units.

Chocolate,
salmon and whisky
are the UK's top three
food and drink exports.

In January 1205,
it was so cold in England that
wine and ale froze and
were sold by weight,
not volume.

The US's ninth-largest brewery
has made a new beer from
recycled sewage water.

In Finland,
you can buy
a party pack of
1,000 cans of beer.

In Sweden,
you can buy
toilet paper called
Kräpp.

The original patent
for the toilet-roll holder
showed the paper hanging
over the holder,
not under.

Post-it notes
should be peeled with
the sticky strip vertical,
not horizontal.

Wrapping paper
is only 100
years old.

1 in 100
Americans
work for Walmart.

FTSE 100 CEOs
make more money
in two and a half days
than the average worker
makes in a year.

Only 4.2% of
Fortune 500 companies
are run by women.

Men appear
in the newspapers
three times as often as women
and have done so
since 1800.

During the Second World War,
Women's Institutes played
'Pin the Moustache on Hitler'.

In the Second World War,
it was illegal to post
knitting patterns abroad
in case they contained
coded messages.

In 1857,
British officials were
convinced Indian villagers
were passing secret messages
hidden in chapattis.

The first editorial assistant to
work on the *Oxford English Dictionary*
was sacked for industrial
espionage.

My Adventures as a Spy,
by Lord Baden-Powell, has a chapter on
'The Value of Being Stupid'.

Secret agents have
to be trained to forget
their advanced driving courses.

The CIA
uses board games
to train spies.

The CIA Museum
in Langley, Virginia,
is not open to
the public.

In the First World War,
battlefield observation stations
were hidden inside
trees.

The oak is
the national tree of
Bulgaria, Croatia, Cyprus, Estonia,
France, Germany, Latvia, Lithuania,
Moldova, Poland, Romania,
Serbia and the UK.

There are more trees on Earth
than stars in the
Milky Way.

1% of
all the timber
sold in the world
is bought by IKEA.

12% of
all the iron in
Britain in the 1780s
was cast by one man –
John 'Iron Mad' Wilkinson.

One-third of
entrepreneurs think
their chance of failing
is zero.

'Entopreneurs'
are people who farm
new types of edible insect.

Minecraft
is used to pitch for
business deals.

After shaking hands,
most people unwittingly
sniff their fingers.

Octopuses
smell with
their arms.

Vegetarians
smell nicer than
people who eat meat.

Sniffing milk
to test its freshness
rather than going by
the sell-by date would
save 100 million
pints a year.

In 1946,
only 2% of British
households had
a fridge.

Octopuses spend
3% of their time
tidying.

Only 4% of people
who try to quit smoking
without help succeed.

Only 5% of
Chinese people
have a passport.

31% of
Chinese tourists
pack instant noodles
when they travel.

The ancient Chinese
could count up to a million
on their hands.

Six million years ago,
otters were bigger
than leopards.

An analysis of
eight million books published
between 1776 and 2009
found that Britons
were happiest
in 1957.

In 1957,
the US air force flew
around the world to
show they could bomb
anywhere they wanted.

More than
2,400 nuclear bombs
have been detonated
since 1945.

It will be another 500 years
before the Somme is
free of bombs.

On 16 March 1945,
bombs dropped by the British
on Würzburg, Germany, destroyed
90% of the buildings
in 20 minutes.

90%
of Vietnamese
share just 14 surnames.

90%
of lobsters
escape from lobster traps.

90%
of film critics
are male.

90%
of world trade
is carried by ship.

The world's heaviest aeroplane
weighs as much as the statue
Christ the Redeemer
in Rio de Janeiro.

Until 1970, United Airlines
had 'men only' flights serving
steaks, brandy and cigars.

French tennis player
Suzanne Lenglen drank brandy
between sets but won
98% of her games.

Emma Martina Luigia Morano,
the world's oldest person
when she died at 117, outlived
90 Italian governments.

In 2017,
a Brazilian great-grandmother
discovered the figure of St Anthony
that she'd prayed to for years
was actually an elf from
The Lord of the Rings.

Facebook uses
The Lord of the Rings
to teach its software
how to think.

25% of Americans
think God decides who
wins the Super Bowl.

A ticket to the
first Super Bowl cost $12;
today's tickets cost
up to $3,000.

One side
of the new £1 coin
was designed by
a 15-year-old.

The first Christmas stamp
in the UK was designed
by a six-year-old.

Santa Claus's
first commercial appearance
was in a 1923 advert
for ginger beer.

To visit every
child in the world
Santa would need to travel at
3,000 times the speed of sound.

92% of
shopping-mall Santas
have had their beard pulled
to see if it was real.

30% of shopping-mall Santas
have been urinated on
by a child.

Leopard urine
smells like popcorn.

The Romans used urine
to clean their teeth.

Oxford University's
first professor of chemistry
thought fossils were frozen urine.

If you pick up a desert tortoise,
it can urinate itself
to death.

Most of the white sand
in the Caribbean is made of
parrotfish droppings.

Kangaroos
keep cool by
licking their forearms.

Birds can tell
what the speed limits
are on roads.

The French air force
has a squad of golden eagles,
trained to hunt down
drones.

Dragonflies
can be used as drones
by fitting them with
tiny backpacks.

Japanese scientists
have invented a
robot bee.

The White House
only got the ability to
print double-sided
in 2016.

Lyndon B. Johnson
had a nozzle fitted to his
shower in the White House
that fired water at
his genitals.

Donald Trump
presses a red button
on his desk when he wants
the White House butler to
bring him a Diet Coke.

Domino's customers
can place an order by
tweeting a pizza emoji.

The world's largest pizza
was twice the size
of a tennis court.

From 1974 to 1992,
a third of all tennis Grand Slams
were won by Swedish men;
today, there are none
in the top 150.

A Swede born with
'a silver spoon in their mouth'
is said to have 'slid in on a
shrimp sandwich'.

The Polish equivalent of
'Were you born yesterday?' is
'Did you fall from a
Christmas tree?'

The money spent
on Christmas presents in the UK
could fund the NHS from Boxing Day
to 12 February.

Christmas crackers
were originally called
'bangs of expectation'.

The first Christmas tree
erected in Trafalgar Square
was transported at night because
it exceeded the legal weight limits
on British roads in daytime.

In the Australian outback,
there is a road used for
testing supercars that
has no speed limit.

Potholes in roads
in 19th-century Argentina
were filled with surplus
sheep's heads.

In 19th-century America,
roads were paved with
oyster shells.

An oyster thief
in 19th-century London
called Dando would eat dozens
of oysters, then abscond
without paying.

The Oyster card
was designed by
Saatchi & Saatchi.

Wig-snatching
was a common crime
in 18th-century
England.

In 2014,
German police issued a fine
to a one-armed cyclist
for cycling with
one arm.

The Olympic Village
for the 1980 Winter Games
in Upstate New York is
now a prison.

South Korean sniffer dogs
sold to the Russian police in Siberia
have proved to be useless because
they don't like the cold.

More than a third
of the 8.5 million dogs
in Britain are
obese.

In Taiwan,
it is illegal to walk a dog
by attaching its lead to
a car or motorbike.

Ships are not classified
as abandoned if there is a dog
or a cat onboard.

10,000 shipping containers
are lost from ships
every year.

The largest cruise ships
have a greater population than
the City of London.

Dangerous maritime goods
include pistachios, almonds, walnuts,
hazelnuts, Brazil nuts and peanuts
because they can all self-heat
and spontaneously combust.

There are more than
500 peanuts in the average jar
of peanut butter.

Prince Charles wants to
reduce grey squirrel numbers
by feeding them contraceptives
hidden in Nutella.

Tanzanians scare off elephants
by bombarding them
with condoms filled
with chilli powder.

To treat mites,
beekeepers dust their bees
with sugar.

Honeybees
'whoop' when
they bump into each other.

Bees
can be taught to
play football.

Apes are
the only animals that
need to be taught
how to swim.

The *Mola mola* is
known as the sunfish in English
and the moonfish
in Russian.

The first treadmill on the
International Space Station
was ejected into space
and burned up in
the atmosphere.

Treadmills
were once the
harshest punishment
short of the death penalty.

60% of the
world's selfie deaths
take place in India.

Mahatma Gandhi Pires,
Marlon Brando da Silveira,
John Lennon Silva Santos
and Yago Pikachu are all
Brazilian footballers.

North Korea
is a hereditary
Marxist monarchy.

The Indonesian flag
is the same as the Polish flag
upside down.

Polish is the
second most common language
spoken in the UK.

A clock's
second hand is
really its third hand.

All mammals,
regardless of size,
take 12 seconds
to defecate.

The US State Department
is located in Foggy Bottom.

Eight billion particles of fog
can fit into a
teaspoon.

China's Er Wang Dong cave
is so big it has its own
weather system.

Lightning heats
the surrounding air to
temperatures five times hotter
than the surface of the Sun.

When it gets hot,
normally carnivorous
tadpoles become
vegetarian.

The world's smallest frog
is the size of a
housefly.

The world's tiniest reptile
is a chameleon the
size of an ant.

In 2016,
a new species of ant
was discovered after it was
vomited up by
a frog.

Nymphister kronaueri
is a beetle whose camouflage
makes it look like an
ant's bottom.

In 2004,
a pine tree planted
in memory of George Harrison
died after an infestation
of beetles.

Natural history museums
use teams of beetles
to clean the flesh
off specimens.

Caterpillars
contain more protein
than dung beetles.

John Adams,
second president of the US,
liked to inspect London's dung.

Richard Nixon once
ordered a nuclear strike
on North Korea
when drunk.

In 1987,
Richard Nixon's wife
predicted that Donald Trump
would one day become
the president.

Donald Trump
uses double-sided sticky tape
to hold his tie in place.

Calvin Coolidge
had two pet lions
called Tax Reduction
and Budget Bureau.

Aged 14, Fidel Castro
wrote to President Roosevelt
to ask for $10.

The US Treasury
has a 'Conscience Fund'
for voluntary donations from
people feeling guilty about
cheating on their taxes.

Collectively,
Americans take
300,000 years to do
their tax returns
every year.

A 17th-century Scottish tax
on having sex out of
wedlock was called
'buttock mail'.

Grooflins
is Scots for
flat on one's face.

Whummle
is Scots for
head over heels.

Wabbit
is Scots for exhausted
or slightly unwell.

Snoozle
is Scots for
poke with the nose.

Hitting the snooze button
makes you more tired
during the day.

People who
play the didgeridoo
snore less.

Vitamin B6
helps you remember
your dreams.

Black Americans
don't sleep as well as
white Americans.

In 2017,
six Chinese officials
were punished for falling asleep
in a meeting about how to motivate
lazy bureaucrats.

Inemuri,
or falling asleep in public,
is considered a sign of diligence
in Japanese employees.

Japanese scientists
have warned that people
making the peace sign could have
their fingerprints stolen.

30,000 napkins a month
are stolen from Jamie Oliver's
restaurants.

A statue of Hercules
in Arcachon, France, has had
its penis stolen so often it's been
given a detachable one for
'special occasions'.

In 2012,
thieves in the Czech Republic
stole a 10-tonne railway bridge,
claiming they were clearing
the way for a cycle path.

In 2008,
thieves in Jamaica
stole an entire beach.

The Tamil word for
'stealing a beach' is
manarkollai.

In 2017,
an Irish beach that had
been washed away in 1984
was returned by a
freak tide.

The Hebridean island of Barra
has the only airport in the world
that uses a beach
as a runway.

Qatar Airways
allows up to six falcons to
sit in Economy Class.

Planes
carrying the Pope
use the call sign
'Shepherd One'.

'Playing chess with the Pope'
is an Icelandic euphemism
for having a poo.

The Icelandic word
used for Darth Vader
translates as
'Blackhead'.

From 1966 to 1987,
Iceland banned TV on Thursdays,
to encourage people to get out
and socialise more.

1% of the static
on an untuned TV
is radiation from the
birth of the universe.

The Milky Way produces
nine trillion kilos of antimatter
every second.

Exoplanet HAT-P-7b
has clouds made of
liquid rubies.

29 of the 52
spacecraft sent to Mars
have failed to reach
their destination.

Saturn's
newest moon
is called
Peggy.

The ancient Egyptians had
a hieroglyph for
'meteorite'.

If an asteroid hit the Earth,
only 3% of people would be killed
by the actual impact.

25 million meteors
fall to Earth every day.

You can find
micro-meteorites in
the gutters of European cities.

Birds that live in the city
start tweeting earlier
to avoid rush hour.

Male cockatoos
use drum solos to
attract mates.

In the 17th century,
migrating birds were
thought to go to
the Moon for
winter.

Cities are hotter
from Monday to Friday
and cooler at the
weekend.

Utepils is
Norwegian for
a beer enjoyed outside
on a sunny day.

Muckibus means
'drunkenly sentimental'.

Schnapsidee
is German for an
ingenious plan concocted
while drunk.

The German aristocrat
who invented mulled wine
also invented an
aphrodisiac
sorbet.

Philematology
is the study of
kissing.

Your lips are 1,000 times
more sensitive than
your fingertips.

Ants
communicate by
sharing saliva.

Kissing
under the mistletoe
began between 1720 and 1784,
but nobody knows
exactly when.

Victorian
Christmas trees
were topped with
Union Jacks.

The 'mas'
in Christmas
means 'go away'.

60% of the world's
Christmas decorations
are made in a single
town in China.

For Christmas 2008,
Becks bought Posh
a $100,000
handbag.

Vanilla is
more expensive
than silver.

The Doge of Venice
marries the sea once a year
by throwing a ring
into the water.

Italian scientists
have grown strawberries
in underwater greenhouses
on the seabed.

Vanuatu
has an underwater
post office.

American Express
used to be a delivery company.

Shell
used to sell
shells.

Samsung
began as a
grocery store.

Lamborghini
started out making
tractors.

Drivers in Moscow
spend 25% of their time
in traffic jams.

Britain's roads
are in worse condition
than those of Oman,
Malaysia, Ecuador
and Namibia.

The first car
in Antarctica
didn't work because it
kept overheating.

A car fuelled by
the waste coffee produced
by Caffè Nero in London in a year
could go round the M25
3,689 times.

Voltaire
drank 50 cups of coffee
every day.

Bach
wrote a cantata
about coffee.

Liszt
drank a bottle of cognac
every day.

Kafka
wanted to write
budget travel guides
but couldn't find anyone
to fund them.

In 2017, a Kiwi tourist
was detained in Kazakhstan
because the immigration authorities
refused to believe there was a
country called New Zealand.

1 in 3 parents
allow their children to
choose where to go
on holiday.

45% of British families with children
communicate by text
even when they're
all at home.

Kindergarten children
in Alaska are taught how to
butcher a moose.

It is illegal
in Saudi Arabia
to name a child
Sandi.

It is illegal in Sweden
to name a child
Veranda.

In 2008,
a pair of twins in
New Zealand were named
Benson and Hedges.

Ed Sheeran
can fit 55 Maltesers
into his mouth.

The word 'confetti'
comes from the Italian for
'sugared almonds'.

The US once required
people to have blood tests
before they could marry.

In Britain
in the Second World War,
there was a threefold increase
in bigamy.

In Denmark,
if you're unmarried at 25,
your friends will ambush you
with a cinnamon shower.

Chilli peppers
taste milder in space
than on Earth.

The synthetic drug spice
was originally developed
as a fertiliser for
bonsai trees.

In 2017,
the original
Bramley apple tree
was still living at
207 years old.

Scientists have
found a way to grow
human ears
on apples.

There is no such thing
as a wild orange.

Orang-utans
plan their journeys in advance
and tell friends where
they're going.

Hsing Hsing,
an orang-utan in Perth Zoo,
is attracted to Nicole Kidman.

Sandra,
an orang-utan in Buenos Aires Zoo,
is the first non-human to
become a legal
person.

Three of the world's
rivers are legal persons:
they have guardians and are
treated as minors in court.

More than 90%
of all jury trials in the world
occur in the US.

US lawyers
aren't allowed to
use the words 'honey'
or 'darling' in court.

Swearing on the Bible
is theologically problematic
as the New Testament forbids
the taking of oaths.

Swearing uses
a different part of the brain
to other speech.

In the 14th century,
the name Peter was
a mild swear word.

Brahms once got drunk
and used a word so shocking
it broke up the party and
no one would
repeat it.

Tolstoy wrote in his diary:
'I've fallen in love or imagine I have;
went to a party and lost my head.
Bought a horse which
I don't need at all.'

The Roman consul Crassus
loved his pet eel so much he
bought it necklaces
and earrings.

Tyrannosaurus rex had
a sensitive nose it
probably used for
nuzzling.

The great grey shrike
impales its prey on sharp thorns,
then presents the 'kebab'
to potential mates.

Madagascar hissing cockroaches
can either grow big horns to
fight for a mate or grow
big testicles for mating.
They can't do both.

You aren't allowed
to warm your balls
during a round of golf,
but you can before
you start.

Golfers in
Coober Pedy, Australia,
use glow-in-the-dark balls
because it's so hot by day that
everyone plays at night.

Burglars always
knock on the door before
breaking into a house.

Houses in Vermont
have windows that are
slanted diagonally to stop
witches getting in.

Inuit people
made windows from
walrus penises.

The Queen
has a personal bagpiper
who plays outside her window
for 15 minutes each morning.

The word 'window'
replaced an Old English word
that literally meant
'eye-hole'.

The White House
has 147 windows.

Richard Nixon's chair
was 2.5 inches higher
than everyone else's
in the Cabinet Room.

A throttlebottom is
an inept politician.

A quockerwodger was
a 19th-century politician
whose strings were pulled
by someone else.

Whipmegorum
is a Scots word for a
noisy quarrel about
politics.

Voice dystonia
is the inability to speak
to other people.

Your inner monologue
runs at 67 words
per second.

Artificial speech-
generation software can learn
to sing as well as a person
in 35 minutes.

One of the world's first robots
was Squee the Squirrel,
built in 1951.

CERN has
an animal shelter
for computer mice.

Malmö, Sweden,
has two tiny shops
for mice.

Mice sigh
up to 40 times
an hour.

A Komodo dragon's tongue
can taste its prey from
two and a half
miles away.

Diners spend
£2 more per head
if a restaurant plays
classical music instead of pop.

Listening to music
can change the taste
of wine and toffee.

'I Will Survive', 'Stayin' Alive'
and 'Another One Bites the Dust'
have the correct number
of beats per minute
to perform CPR to.

CPR is
successful
only 8% of the time.

You can make
human heart tissue
from spinach.

Artificial blood vessels
can be made with
a candyfloss
machine.

Oxford University
is developing artificial knees
made from spider silk.

Hummingbirds
use spiders' webs
to glue their nests together.

Male sparrows bring
less food back to the nest
if their partner has been
unfaithful.

It takes 60 nests' worth
of duck down to
fill a duvet.

47 species of fungus
live inside
pillows.

April 1st is
International
Pillow Fight Day.

The national sport of Turkey
is oil wrestling.

New Mexico
has an official state question:
'Red or green?'

Swedish
only became Sweden's
official language
in 2009.

Only 7%
of the Chinese can
speak Chinese properly.

In 2010,
Fiji lost its original
Declaration of Independence
and had to ask Britain
for a photocopy.

In 1875,
the Royal Navy erased
123 islands from their charts
because they didn't exist.

In 2001,
the AA had to pay £20 million
after it was caught copying
Ordnance Survey maps.

Google Maps in India
has Kashmir belonging to India.
In Pakistan, it shows it
as being disputed.

In 1983,
the Spanish town of Lijar
ended its 100-year war with France
due to 'the excellent attitude
of the French'.

More people
visit France than
any other country
on Earth.

The happiest country
in the world is
Costa Rica.

The friendliest country
in the world is
Iceland.

In Japan,
police carry
massive futons
to roll up drunks in.

Korobikobou is
Japanese police slang for
deliberately bumping into a suspect
and then arresting them
for obstruction.

All Japanese police officers
are expected to become
a black belt in judo.

Police in Zambia
are not allowed to marry
foreigners.

The neon flying squid
is faster than
Usain Bolt.

The scientific name
for the black bee-fly is
Anthrax anthrax.

The pom-pom crab
carries sea anemones in its claws
and waves them around
when threatened.

A group
of cockroaches
is called an
'intrusion'.

Slugs
are twice as fast
as snails.

Rats practise
walking and running
before they're
born.

At the first Olympics,
athletes got a bronze medal
just for taking part.

The winner of the
1896 Olympic discus competition
had never thrown a
discus before.

Croquet was
dropped as an Olympic sport
after the 1900 games, when
only one spectator
turned up.

The Rio Olympics
employed 75 lifeguards at
the swimming events.

600 million years ago,
the Earth's oceans were
freshwater.

Swedish scientists
have discovered that
water is a combination of
two distinct forms
of liquid.

Dolphins
provide babysitting
services.

Smooth-fan lobsters
travel inside jellyfish
and eat them as
they go.

Lobsters' brains
are the same size
as the tip of a ballpoint pen.

Healthy human brains
feel like warm
scallops.

Your brain
dries out as you age.

The UK has four times
as many people aged over 100
as it had 30 years ago.

An 'oldster'
was a Royal Navy term
for a midshipman of
four years' standing.

The giant shipworm
grows as tall as a
12-year-old
child.

In 2017,
Doris Day discovered
she was two years older than
she thought she was.

Julius Caesar
wanted to ban actors
from holding public office.

In 168 BC,
the only tradesmen in Rome
who were not slaves
were bakers.

In 14th-century London,
the Bakers Guild split up and
formed two rival guilds:
one for brown bread
and one for white.

In Venezuela,
90% of all wheat
must be made into bread
rather than cakes or pastries.

In Waitrose,
it costs more to buy
empty jam jars than
ones with jam in.

Houses in Britain
numbered 13 cost
£9,000 less than average.

Million Dollar Point
is an area in the Pacific where the
US army dumped all its equipment
after the Second World War
because it was cheaper
than bringing it home.

The sailfish
can swim at
70 mph.

Swordfish
secrete oil from their noses
to smooth their passage
through the water.

An oyster
can filter 50 gallons
of water a day.

Most fish food
is made of
fish.

Fish sing
the dawn chorus.

British children can be
held responsible for crimes
from the age of 10, but
can't own a goldfish
until they're 16.

In medieval England,
you could be made an outlaw
if you failed to turn up to court
five times in a row.

It is illegal in France
to breed killer whales
in captivity.

A pod of killer whales
breathes in unison
while asleep.

The zombie worm
lives and feeds on the
bones of whales.

The Swedish for 'whale'
also means
'election'.

Parliamentary elections in India
are three times as likely to be won
by politicians convicted of
serious crimes.

Ochlocracy
is democracy's evil twin:
rule by the mob.

In seven US states,
you can change your vote
after you've cast it.

Pennsylvanian candidates
in the 2016 US presidential election
included Mickey Mouse, Wonder Woman,
Harambe the Gorilla, Richard Nixon,
We Deserve Better and
Shoot Me Now.

Nevada is the only state
whose ballot papers have
a 'None of the above' option.

Scientists in Massachusetts
have invented an AI machine
that can see two seconds
into the future.

Beijing has
three million hens
that are looked after
by robot nannies.

Dubai police
have a Robocop.

The US Department of Defense
still uses 8-inch
floppy disks.

The first aircraft carriers
were designed to carry
hot-air balloons.

Balloons and helicopters
frighten the meerkats in London Zoo,
but aeroplanes and pigeons
don't.

Pigeons
can be trained to
identify breast cancer.

Rats can
diagnose tuberculosis
faster than doctors.

In the 16th century,
cancer was thought to be
curable with tobacco.

In the 17th century,
Greek monks thought
that tobacco was the
excrement of Satan.

In the 18th century,
gin was thought to cure
seasickness.

In the 19th century,
an Edinburgh doctor sold
homeopathic snake excrement
to treat chest problems.

Russia has
800,000 faith healers but
only 640,000 doctors.

Traces of aspirin
and penicillin have been
found on the teeth of
Neanderthals.

Neanderthals
ate rhinoceroses.

Buddha
was not fat.

During the Second World War,
British pilots carried chocolate bars
infused with garlic in case they were
shot down and needed to make
their breath smell French.

Eating garlic
improves your
body odour.

You can buy cologne
that smells of
Play-Doh.

Rats
can smell fear.

Naked mole-rats
can survive for 18 minutes
without oxygen by turning
themselves into plants.

Cuttlefish
change colour to
elude predators but
are themselves
colour-blind.

Side-blotched lizards have
three throat colours
and five genders.

The thorny devil lizard
drinks through
its skin.

Ostriches
don't drink at all;
they get all the water
they need from the
plants they eat.

Water in
Chile's Atacama Desert has
100 times the safe level of arsenic,
but local people have evolved
to process it.

73% of people
who are allergic to pollen
are also allergic to
cannabis.

Neurotic people
are more likely to
see faces in random objects.

Because of the way
their eyes are positioned,
pigs can't see
the sky.

Starfish
have eyes on
the tips of their arms.

The cockeyed squid
has one regular-sized eye
and one giant eye.

The box jellyfish
has 24 eyes, some of which
always look skywards,
even when it is
upside down.

The Portuguese man-o'-war jellyfish
is hunted by the blanket octopus, which
rips off its poisonous tentacles and
uses them as weapons.

Gloomy octopuses
throw seashells
at each other.

Octopuses
range in size from
two centimetres
to six metres
across.

Dolphins
tenderise octopuses
by bashing them around
before eating them.

The defence mechanism of
turkey vultures is to
vomit up their
last meal.

King ratsnakes,
or 'stinking goddesses',
deter predators by
emptying their
anal glands.

Opossums
defend themselves
by faking their own death.

The UK spends
less on defence than
it does paying interest on
the national debt.

1 in 14 Britons
is on an NHS waiting list.

10% of the NHS budget
is used to treat
diabetes.

97% of people
visiting hospital with appendicitis
report pain when going
over speed bumps
on the way.

The world's hottest chilli
was bred to be used
as an anaesthetic.

15% of the air
on the New York subway
contains human skin.

The Brazilian wax
was invented in
New York.

The high five
was invented
in 1977.

Before
the invention of
pressurised cabins,
all airline passengers
had to wear oxygen masks.

Wealthy women in the 16th century
wore black velvet masks
to protect their faces
from the sun.

Japanese farmers
protect the pale flesh of
melons from sunburn
by putting small
hats on them.

The hooded nudibranch
is a sea slug that smells
like watermelon.

Sea lions
love the smell of
cinnamon.

Whale breath
smells like a mixture
of fish and farts.

Liver failure
makes your breath smell
of raw fish.

German measles
makes your sweat smell
of freshly plucked
feathers.

Typhoid
makes your skin smell of
freshly baked bread.

One outbreak of
Legionnaires' disease
was traced to the hot tub in
the Playboy Mansion.

The Playboy Mansion
has the second-largest
residential pipe organ
in the US.

Until the 16th century,
many people carried
tiny portable organs
called 'organetti'.

Half of churchgoers
have noticed an organist
slipping in unexpected tunes
during a service.

Any song
played on the radio in
1940s America had to have
the whole band present
in the studio.

Paul McGuigan,
the original bassist in Oasis,
quit the band by fax.

1 in 5 British households
own a vinyl copy of *Sgt Pepper's
Lonely Hearts Club Band*.

The composer
who sold the most
music CDs in 2016 was
Wolfgang Amadeus Mozart.

Opera Helps
sends opera singers
round to your house to sing
the appropriate aria for
your problems.

Jacques Offenbach gave his operas
long overtures because people
were often late for the
performances.

Tchaikovsky
wanted his *1812 Overture*
to be played with live cannons.

Tchaikovsky said
the *1812 Overture* was
'very loud and noisy and completely
without artistic merit, obviously written
without warmth or love'.

In 2009,
Vodafone recreated
the *1812 Overture* using
ringtones from 1,000
mobile phones.

Mobile-phone users
in the Netherlands are provided with
traffic lights on the pavement to
stop them getting run over.

Prozvonit is
a Czech word meaning
'to call someone's mobile
so they have your number'.

Phubbing
is a new word meaning
'ignoring your friends in favour
of your mobile phone'.

The more crowded
a subway train gets,
the more people buy things
on their phones.

The number of
shopping centres in
North Korea doubled
between 2010
and 2017.

Papua New Guinea
has only recognised Taiwan
for one week
in 1999.

Books may not
enter or leave Tajikistan
without written permission
from the Ministry of Culture.

Google has a database of
25 million books that nobody
is allowed to read.

The Little Prince,
by Antoine de Saint-Exupéry,
is the first non-religious book to
be translated into
300 languages.

A Coptic translation
of the New Testament is
the world's slowest-selling book:
the first print run of 500 copies
took 191 years to sell.

A library book
borrowed by George Washington
in 1789 wasn't returned
until 2010.

The British Library
keeps its collection of
over 60 million newspapers in
an airtight room with low oxygen
so they can't catch fire.

The Moon
has been collecting
tiny bits of the Earth for
three billion years.

Collectively,
humans have watched
Adam Sandler movies on Netflix
for longer than civilisation
has existed.

Netflix's
biggest competitor
is sleep.

In 2017,
an Australian MP
laughed so hard at
the US TV show *Veep*
he knocked himself out.

The two biggest
opening-week releases
in South Korean film history
were both horror movies.

On the first day of filming,
Colin Farrell always wears his
lucky shamrock-patterned
underpants.

Tony Blair wore
the same pair of shoes for every
Prime Minister's Questions
for 10 years.

In JFK's
first political campaign,
a newspaper complained he was
'ever so British'.

The US Constitution
is kept in an atomic-
bomb-proof
vault.

The Indian judiciary
has a backlog of
31 million
cases.

Mumbai
has the world's
highest concentration
of leopards.

The world's highest concentration
of peregrine falcons is in
New York City.

In Alabama,
it is illegal to wear
a fake moustache that
causes laughter in church.

It is illegal in China to
use the national anthem
as your ringtone.

In Iran,
it is illegal to
walk a dog.

Popes John I, John X,
John XI and John XIV
all died in prison.

Pope Leo X
told a man with
17,000 holy relics
that he had saved himself
694,779,550 days in purgatory.

During the 1914 Christmas truce,
German troops put up a sign that said
'*Gott mitt uns*', meaning 'God with us'.
A British sign in response read:
'We got mittens too'.

Volkswagen's
official language
is not German
but English.

The Chinese
buy more electric cars
than everyone else in the
world combined.

The maps used
by self-driving cars
cannot be read
by humans.

Rolls-Royce
added the Spirit of Ecstasy
to the bonnets of its cars
to stop drivers using
tasteless mascots.

In the 1980s,
Nissan's talking cars
used tiny vinyl records.

At 19th-century funerals
the last words of the dying were
often played on early
gramophones.

Alexander Graham Bell's
Ear Phonautograph was a
recording device using
a real human ear
from a corpse.

John Logie Baird
called his prototype television
a 'shadowgraph'.

Jeremy Clarkson's
The Grand Tour on Amazon is
the most illegally watched
TV show ever.

It takes 18 people
900 hours to put out
the red carpet for
the Oscars.

The man who won
the Oscar for best screenplay
for *The Bridge on the River Kwai* was
a Frenchman who couldn't
speak or write
English.

Jerry Lewis
is known in France as
Le Roi du Crazy.

The first
named individual in history
was an accountant.

More species have been
named after Barack Obama than
any other US president.

Neopalpa donaldtrumpi
is a moth named after Donald Trump
that has blond hair and
comes from Mexico.

Words used by
Donald Trump for the first time
in a US president's inaugural address
include 'bleed', 'ripped', 'rusted', 'stolen',
'trapped' and 'tombstones'.

Donald Trump
got tens of thousands of dollars
in tax breaks by using goats to
cut the grass on his
golf courses.

Emperor Wu,
the first emperor of China,
visited his harem in a goat cart;
whoever the goats stopped beside
was chosen as his concubine.

Angora goats are
named after the old spelling
of the Turkish capital,
Ankara.

Goats are accepted
at schools in Zimbabwe
in lieu of tuition fees.

The only woman
in Einstein's physics class
at Zürich Polytechnic
married him.

A peer-reviewed paper
on low-temperature physics
was published in 1975
by a cat.

A 1998 study
found cats prefer
cat lovers to cat haters.

64% of Americans
prefer their cat's company
to their partner's.

Dog lovers tend to have
more Facebook friends than cat lovers,
but cat lovers get invited
to more parties.

Most female cats
are right-pawed,
and most male cats
are left-pawed.

Most orang-utans
are left-handed, but
most gorillas and chimpanzees
are right-handed.

In 2016,
a gorilla escaped at London Zoo
and drank five litres of
blackcurrant squash.

One of the first
chimpanzees in London Zoo
came from Bristol by
overnight coach.

Zoo animals
have specially made
toothbrushes.

Naked mole-rats
operate their front teeth
like chopsticks.

Ocelots
don't have any chewing teeth,
so they have to swallow
their food whole.

Straightening
people's teeth
also improves
their balance.

In 2011,
a Canadian dentist bought
one of John Lennon's teeth
at auction for
£19,000.

In 2017,
British doctors found
27 lost contact lenses in
a patient's eye.

The average person
farts 14 times
a day.

The weights
in a gym have
362 times more bacteria
than a toilet seat.

Ocean bacteria
drift into the sky
in spray and help
create clouds.

Most of
'The Cloud'
is underwater.

All the cables
under the ocean
joined together would
be long enough to reach
to the Moon
and back.

Google reinforced
its undersea cables because
they kept being nibbled
by sharks.

40% of a shark's brain
is dedicated to its
sense of smell.

Female Greenland sharks
reach sexual maturity
at 150 years old.

Humpback whales
protect other species from
killer whales.

Killer whales'
favourite delicacy is
whale's tongue.

Coral's main source
of nutrition is
fish pee.

The world's
tallest church is
being eroded by men
urinating on it.

Two churches on
the Greek island of Chios
celebrate Easter by firing
rockets at each other.

In 1579,
English pirates raided
and destroyed a Spanish ship,
mistaking its cargo of cocoa beans
for sheep droppings.

Sheep-creeps are
low, square openings in
drystone walls that let sheep in
but keep cattle out.

Cows lie down
when it's cold or
when they're tired,
not necessarily when
it's about to rain.

A bull named
Pawnee Farm Arlinda Chief
has more than two million
great-granddaughters.

Shakespeare's
daughter Judith was
excommunicated.

Only four people
went to Jane Austen's
funeral.

George Eliot's
right hand was much
bigger than her left.

George Bernard Shaw
left money in his will to
fund a 40-letter
alphabet.

George Orwell
said beer was best drunk
out of china cups.

A thirsty camel
can drink a pint in
3.25 seconds.

It would take
23 bales of straw
to break a camel's back.

Abu Dhabi
has a beauty contest
for camels.

In 1758,
two camels came to London,
one with one hump and one with two.
They were called 'the surprising camel'
and 'the wonderful camel'.

The first pharaoh
of a united Egypt was
killed by a hippo.

There is only one
deaf dentist
in Egypt.

In 2016,
an Egyptian government memo
on how to crush the press
was accidentally sent
to the press.

In 1966,
the Chinese press claimed
Chairman Mao swam nine miles
down the Yangtze in 65 minutes,
making him twice as fast
as Michael Phelps.

Michael Phelps's training breakfast
consisted of an omelette, porridge,
three slices of French toast,
three egg sandwiches
and three pancakes.

Tea leaves
can flow upstream
from the cup
to the pot.

A tablespoonful
of oil dropped into a lake can
calm half an acre of water.

Adulterated olive oil
makes three times as much
profit as cocaine.

The fashion
for heavily oiled hair in
Victorian times is the reason
for headrest cloths
on trains.

18th-century
hairstyles included
Spaniel's Ears, Mad Dog
and The Drowned Chicken.

A 16th-century
recipe for an omelette included
clover, goat's cheese, cinnamon, mint,
spring onion, marjoram, nutmeg
and pig's blood.

Pigs
can be
pessimistic.

Rats have
near-death
experiences.

Ravens
suffer from
paranoia.

Egyptian fruit bats
argue.

Glow-worms
go fishing.

Merlin
was a Slytherin.

The Hobbit
contains only one
instance of the word
'she'.

The words
'girl' and 'boy' appear
only once each
in the Bible.

The Bible's
Wikipedia entry
has fewer citations
than the one for
Pokémon Go.

There are
more positions
in a game of Go than
there are atoms in
the universe.

The European Parliament
recommends chess is played
in all schools.

In medieval chess,
each pawn had its own role:
Gambler, City Guard, Innkeeper,
Merchant, Doctor, Weaver,
Blacksmith and Farmer.

In the 1930s,
there were five suits in
a pack of cards.

Gamblers in Japan
are only allowed to bet
on horse, boat or cycle races.

Less than 1%
of sports bets in the US
are placed legally.

All forms of gambling
were illegal in Russia for
60 years from
1928 to 1988.

In 1913,
the roulette wheel
in Monte Carlo came up black
26 times in a row.

The Queen Mother's funeral
was rehearsed for
22 years.

Guillermo del Toro
does all his writing in a room
with a fake thunderstorm
going on outside.

The longest known lightning bolt
could have reached from
Brussels to London.

There are as many
Russian agents in London
today as there were
at the height of
the Cold War.

The location of
the Teletubbies set
was so secret that visitors
had to be blindfolded.

The average person
has 13 secrets.

'Eleven Men and a Secret'
was the Brazilian version
of *Ocean's Eleven*.

In China,
Pretty Woman became
'I Will Marry a Prostitute
to Save Money'.

The original
Godzilla costume
was made of concrete.

All Quiet on the Western Front
was banned in Poland for
being pro-German and
in Germany for being
anti-German.

$1,000 Reward (1913),
a film about escaping convicts,
was banned in Britain in case
it gave real convicts ideas.

In Mexico,
it isn't illegal to
escape from prison.

In Greek mythology,
Odysseus escapes the Cyclops
by hiding under a sheep. In the
Apache version, he hides in the
anus of a buffalo.

In case someone
needs to escape a polar bear,
people in Churchill, Canada,
never lock their
car doors.

Self-driving Volvos
avoid deer, elk and caribou
but don't recognise
kangaroos.

Dutch trains
have laser cannons
to fire at leaves on the line.

On busy Chinese trains,
passengers take turns on the seats
so everyone gets to sit for
some of the journey.

Noise-reduction equipment
on Chinese trains means they make
no more noise than
a dishwasher.

Items left on
British trains include
a six-foot-tall inflatable dinosaur,
a dead fish and a framed photo
of Mary Berry.

Cranberries
cannot be farmed
organically.

Most Americans
have never eaten a
blackcurrant.

The cheapest Big Macs
in the world can be
found in Egypt.

Uzbek master chefs
can cook enough food in
a single cauldron to
feed 1,000 men.

The Estonian army
travels with pop-up
saunas.

Morse code operators
in the Second World War could
recognise each other's 'accents'
over the line.

In January 1945, the Nova Scotia police
received complaints that drivers
were using their horns to send
filthy messages in Morse.

People who swear
are less likely
to be liars.

Rudeness
is contagious.

Kea parrots
find laughter contagious
and high-five in
mid-air.

In 2017,
a parrot thief in Taiwan
handed himself in because he
couldn't cope with the
incessant squawking.

Male kakapo parrots
have a mating call that can
be heard four miles away, but
females can't tell where
it's coming from.

Drug-addicted parrots are
depleting India's
opium crop.

Humans have
been using cannabis
for 10,000 years and
dealing in it for
5,000 years.

The first Europeans
known to have tried cannabis
lay on the ground complimenting
each other, before one started
a fight with a pillar.

25% of the
cocaine in the US
arrives by submarine.

British warships
make so much noise that
enemy submarines can hear them
from 100 miles away.

The oldest intact
sunken warship in the US is
called the *Land Tortoise*.

The golden tortoise beetle
turns red when aroused
or threatened.

Saying 'Ow'
when you stub your toe
makes it hurt less.

'Oi'
has been rated
the 61st most beautiful
word in English.

A theist is
someone who
is addicted to tea.

Batrachomymachy
is the technical term for
making a mountain
out of a molehill.

An *eedle-doddle* is
Scots for someone who
shows no initiative
in a crisis.

Sobremesa
is Spanish for the
time spent relaxing and
enjoying the company
after a meal.

Queen Victoria
ate bone marrow
every day.

When dieting,
Queen Victoria ate
what her doctors advised
on top of her normal meals.

Queen Victoria
could read and write
in Urdu and Hindi.

In Urdu and Hindi,
the word for 'panda'
is *panda*.

Pandas
are white so they
can hide in the snow
and black so they can hide
in the shadows.

Foxes in Australia
climb trees to
eat koalas.

When the Queen
toured Australia in 1954,
75% of Australians went to see her.

The Australian coat of arms
features an emu and a kangaroo
because they supposedly
can't go backwards,
but they can.

Mariah Carey
employs a man
to walk backwards
in front of her.

Ostriches
can only kick forwards.

Trap-jaw ants
hit each other with
their antennae more than
40 times a second.

Soldier ants
carry wounded comrades
back to the nest.

US medical
diagnosis code S30.862
deals with insect bites
on the penis.

Code V91.35 is
'hit by a falling object
due to a canoeing accident'.

Code W55.21 is
'bitten by a cow'.

Code V91.07 is
'burn caused by
water skis on fire'.

At an arson trial
in Florida in 2017,
a lawyer's trousers
burst into flames.

Snapdragon
was an old Christmas game
where you grabbed a raisin from
a bowl of burning brandy and
put it in your mouth.

Before turkey was adopted,
the traditional British Christmas meal
was a pig's head and mustard.

For Christmas 2012,
Angelina Jolie gave Brad Pitt
a $1.6 million Californian
waterfall.

Tennyson
once earned 1,000 guineas for
writing a verse for a Christmas card.

Mendelssohn
wrote the tune for
'Hark the Herald Angels Sing'.
He said he didn't mind what the words were
as long as they weren't religious.

Bach
composed the
Brandenburg Concertos
as a job application but
never got a reply.

Liszt
had a stalker who
stole the dregs of his tea and
used it as perfume.

The world's largest perfume archive
is the Osmothèque in Versailles.
It has 4,000 scents dating
back to the 1800s.

The 'Odour of Sanctity' is
the heavenly smell given off
by the bodies of
dead saints.

The smell of the apocalypse
was created by artists in 2016,
using scents mentioned in
the Book of Revelation.

Apocalypse,
Stormageddon, Root Ripper,
Branch Wobbler and In a Teacup
are names for storms suggested
by the British public.

Gluggaveður
('window-weather')
is Icelandic for weather
that looks beautiful but
is best enjoyed from
indoors.

Komorebi
is Japanese for
sunlight filtering
through the trees.

The colours
of rainbows are
used to measure
air pollution.

Los Angeles
has had the same climate
for 50,000 years.

When hot weather comes,
zebra finches sing
to their eggs to
warn them.

A baby partridge
is called a 'cheeper'.

1,400 wrens
weigh as much
as one swan.

A ladybird's wings
are four times the size
of its body.

Three plovers,
a parrot and a baboon
feature in the Scottish version of
'The Twelve Days of Christmas'.

A Victorian time capsule
buried in London contains photographs
of the 12 most beautiful women
in England.

A photo of Nick Clegg was
used in an ad at Las Vegas airport
after the designers thought
it was a stock image.

Mrs Thatcher did
four photo shoots for *Vogue*
and could get ready for them
in four minutes.

The photons
hitting your retina right now
were passing Mercury
five minutes ago.

No man-made object
has survived on Venus
for more than 127 minutes.

Half the water on Earth
is older than
the Sun.

Mars was
once devastated
by 50-metre tsunamis.

Jupiter's Northern Lights
cover an area larger
than Earth.

On Saturn's moon Titan,
twilight is 200 times brighter
than midday.

Uranus doesn't smell much,
apart from the odd
fart-like waft.

The fastest winds
in the universe are
on Neptune.

Pluto
has towers of ice
1,600 feet tall.

Alpine glaciers
are to be stored in a
specially built bunker
in Antarctica.

Types of ice include
pancake, icefoot
and bummock.

ICE,
or Immigration
and Customs Enforcement,
is a US agency that deports
so many people it has
its own airline.

Police in Arizona
must check your immigration status
if called to inspect the height
of your grass.

In Arkansas,
it is illegal for grass
to be six inches tall.

The Washington Monument
was completed in 1888,
but nobody knew its
height until 2015.

The advertising
for Trump World Tower
claims it is 19 floors taller
than it actually is.

Donald Trump
has bathmophobia,
the fear of falling
down stairs.

David Cameron
likes to imagine that
any pheasants he shoots
are called Boris or Michael.

All Margaret Thatcher's
government documents had
different spacing so she would know
who'd leaked one if it appeared
in the press.

Mrs Thatcher slept
for the same number of hours
each night as an elephant.

The US army spent millions
finding out if elephants
could be used to
smell bombs.

At least 61 species
live in elephants'
footprints.

The first giraffe in Britain
was said to have died as a result
of a sympathetic reaction to
gout in George IV's toe.

Robert Cecil,
1st Earl of Salisbury,
fed claret to his
pet parakeet.

Sabrage is a technique
for opening champagne
with a cavalry sword.

A fencing guide from 1763
allowed the use of lanterns
to illuminate opponents,
to dazzle them and
to hit them with.

Yorkshire had
a Christmas tradition
of festive sword dancing.

Only a quarter of employees
look forward to their
Christmas party.

The word 'Xmas'
was in use before the
word 'Christmas'.

The first recipe
for Brussels sprouts
advised buttering them and
serving them on toast.

The world's largest
mince-pie factory can
make two million pies
in 24 hours.

Pie crusts
used to be called
'coffins'.

The award ceremony
for obituary writers is called
'The Grimmies'.

The 2016 Florida Keys
Hemingway Lookalike Contest
was won by Mr Dave Hemingway
(no relation).

A Paul Gascoigne
lookalike competition in
South Shields in 1991 was
won by a teenage girl.

The winner of Australia's 2011
'So You Think You Can Stare' competition
lasted 40 minutes and 59 seconds
without blinking.

Cinema audiences
blink in unison.

The best female golfer
in America putts with
her eyes closed.

One of the only players
on the US PGA golf tour
not to wear a glove
is Lucas Glover.

NASA has a robo-glove
which gives the wearer
three times more
gripping power.

On the Moon,
there's a piece of lava
from Oregon.

Oregon is
the only US state
with a double-sided flag.

The name of
Portland, Oregon,
was chosen by tossing a coin.
The other option was
'Boston'.

In 19th-century Boston,
it was bad luck to cut your nails
at weekends.

Atlanta Zoo
has a cockroach called
Tom Brady.

A cockroach's heart
has 13 chambers.

The world's healthiest
human hearts belong to
the Tsimane people of Bolivia,
who eat monkeys, tapirs,
wild pigs and piranhas.

Rainwater contains
vitamin B12.

Tears contain
vitamin A.

Six-week-old babies cry
for an average of two hours
and 15 minutes a day.

Babies in Britain
cry more than babies in Japan,
and nobody knows why.

Denmark
has more pigs
than people.

Pigs go 'oink'
in Italy and Spain,
'snork' in South Africa,
'groin' in France
and 'buu buu'
in Japan.

The Curly-Coated Lincoln
is an extinct breed of pig that
had a woolly coat
like a sheep.

The world's first
self-service grocery shop
was called Piggly Wiggly.

The world's
biggest shopping mall
has an indoor ski resort and
a penguin colony.

Shops in Bristol are plagued by a
'grammar vigilante' who goes around
correcting misplaced apostrophes
on their sign's.

The most misspelled
word in English is
'separate'.

The word 'nice'
is from the Latin *nescius,*
which means
'ignorant'.

Roald Dahl's
school report said:
'I have never met anybody
who so persistently writes words
meaning the exact opposite
of what is intended.'

Wally
in *Where's Wally?* is
80% smaller than when
he first appeared
in 1987.

The world's smallest bat
weighs as much as
a paper clip.

Vampire bats
chase their prey
on foot.

Bats can swim.

Hippos can't swim;
they stroll about
on the riverbed.

Dumbo octopuses
swim using their large
ear-like protuberances.

The average
public swimming pool
contains enough urine to
fill a dustbin.

Olympic swimmers wear
two swimming caps.

James Madison was
the first US president
to wear trousers.

In the first
two years of his reign,
Henry VII spent £3 million
on clothes.

François Hollande,
the former French president,
spent the equivalent of
£99,000 per year
on haircuts.

Winston Churchill's household
spent £104,400 on
wine each year.

The wine in
a £5 bottle of wine
is worth 47p.

The first
Scottish wine,
produced in 2015,
was described by experts
as 'undrinkable'.

King Zhou of Shang
built a wine lake in China
and made naked men and women
chase each other round it.

There are lakes
under the
sea.

Australia's Pink Lake
has bright-pink
water.

Blood Falls
in Antarctica has
bright-red water that is
so salty it cannot freeze.

The 'ice' on the
first artificial ice rink was
made of pig fat
and salt.

There is
no such thing as
artificial salt.

Small icebergs
are called 'growlers'
because of the sound they
make as they melt.

When the *Titanic*
first hit the iceberg,
passengers played football
with the bits of ice that
fell on the deck.

Mob football,
played in the Middle Ages
between whole towns and villages,
had an unlimited number of players
and a pig's-bladder ball.

French football clubs
cannot hire managers
who are over 65.

Eric Cantona
was banned for a month
for throwing the ball at the referee,
extended to two months after he
told the disciplinary committee
they were idiots.

Stupid people
thinking they are clever
and clever people thinking they aren't
is called the Dunning–Kruger effect.

The Dilbert Principle
is that the worst staff are
put in middle management to
limit the damage they can cause.

The Peter Principle
holds that people are always
promoted beyond their ability.

The crown prince of Thailand
promoted his dog Fufu to
Air Chief Marshal of the
Royal Thai Air Force.

There has only been
one dog in the Royal Navy:
Able Seaman Just Nuisance.

New Zealand police
have a guinea pig mascot
called Constable Elliot.

Juma the Jaguar,
mascot of the 2016 Rio Olympics,
escaped before the games
and was shot dead.

During the first
performance of the play
Harry Potter and the Cursed Child,
an owl got loose and flew out
into the audience.

On Disneyland's opening day,
someone put a ladder in the car park
and charged people $5 to
climb over the hedge.

Popular items for
Amazon customers in
the Andaman Islands are
ladders, brooms and
mayonnaise.

Amazon ships
bubblewrap in bubblewrap.

Container ships contain
basketball courts.

'Monk's balls'
are popular pastries in
Argentina.

The Serbian for 'pride'
means 'diarrhoea'
in Russian.

In Sweden,
'spontaneous dancing'
was illegal until
2017.

The sprinting champion
awarded the laurel wreath at
the first Olympic Games
was a baker.

In 1986,
London's bakers apologised
for the Great Fire of London,
320 years after it happened.

Since 2003,
166 people have fallen
down the gap at Baker Street
Tube station.

Lift operator Betty Lou Oliver
holds the record for the
longest survived fall:
she fell 75 floors.

The world's
fastest elevator
travels at 47 mph.

The Oval Office has
pressure pads under the carpet
so the Secret Service knows exactly
where the president is
at all times.

The 400 men who
carved the presidents
on Mount Rushmore had
their own baseball team.

There's a hidden room
in Mount Rushmore behind
Lincoln's head.

Gustav Eiffel
had a tiny apartment
at the top of the Eiffel Tower
with a grand piano in it.

Hidden inside
Grand Central Station
is the Vanderbilt Tennis Club.

After unexpected rain
during the 1971 Davis Cup,
the tennis court was dried out by
dousing it in petrol and
setting it on fire.

Headis
is table tennis
played with the head
and a small football.

A caterpillar's head
contains 248 muscles.

Caterpillars
retain their memories
when they turn into
moths.

Illacme tobini
is a millipede with
414 legs, 200 poison glands
and four penises.

No centipede
has ever been found
with exactly a hundred legs.

Objects
viewed from
between the legs
look smaller.

Tripod fish
have three legs
and stand at the bottom
of the ocean.

By 2050,
the plastic in
the world's oceans
will outweigh the fish.

Only 20% of fish species
live in the sea.

The Queen bought six
Big Mouth Billy Bass
singing fish for
Balmoral.

The Queen's
90th birthday presents included
a silver Post-it note holder,
an ostrich egg, two stags
and a horse.

It is illegal in the UK
to be drunk in charge
of a horse.

Until 1952,
only male cavalry officers
were permitted to compete in
Olympic equestrian events.

The first event at the Olympic Games
in 396 BC was a trumpet contest:
the winner played the fanfare
for all the other events.

In 2000, a 103-year-old man
returned the official Olympic flag
that he stole as a dare after
coming third in diving at
the 1920 Olympics.

The first American woman
to win an Olympic gold medal
didn't realise she'd entered
the Olympics.

The first female American mayor
was nominated for election
by a group of men
as a joke.

President Obama's
farewell speech mentioned
'democracy' 20 times – more than
the farewell speeches of the
previous 15 presidents
combined.

Barack Obama
has an irrational fear
of snowmen.

Bear Grylls
is scared of
cocktail parties.

Apeirophobia
is the fear of
eternity.

Alogotransiphobia
is the fear of being caught
on public transport without
a book to read.

Books
used to be bound
in otter skin.

Sea otters in China
used to be called 'soft gold',
because their pelts were
so valuable.

80% of
the world's gold is
yet to be found.

Norway's Bouvet Island
is so remote that after it was
discovered in 1739, it was lost again
for another 69 years.

Every year,
Ocean Shores, Washington,
celebrates the night George Vancouver
sailed past their harbour but
didn't discover it.

Geologists
have discovered
an eighth continent off the
coast of Australia.

A cow-smuggling tunnel
has been discovered under the
India–Pakistan border.

Some US farmers
feed their cattle Skittles
because they're cheaper
than corn.

A bank in Zimbabwe
accepts cattle as
collateral.

If you have
£1,785 of savings,
you are richer than half of
the world's population.

2016 was the
first year since 1990
that none of Japan's 4,000
public companies
went bankrupt.

⊙

100,000 Japanese
disappear without trace
every year.

The ghost orchid,
Britain's rarest wild flower,
reappeared 23 years after
being declared
extinct.

Washington DC
is said to be haunted by
DC the Demon Cat.

GCHQ has an internal
ghost-hunting club.

GCHQ code words
for surveillance techniques
include 'nut allergy', 'country file',
'dirty devil' and 'clumsy beekeeper'.

The Pentagon
has six ZIP codes.

Buckingham Palace
has its own
post office.

The Post Office
used to employ cats
to stop mice from eating
money orders.

Thomas Hardy
had a cat called
Kiddleywinkempoops.

Thomas Cromwell
had four pet
beavers.

Thomas Edison
invented the word
'hello'.

Thomas Mann's daughter
adapted a typewriter
so her dog could
write poetry.

The first typewriter was called
'the writing harpsichord'.

In Shakespeare's day, plays were
put on as soon as they were written;
actors rehearsed using 'foul papers',
the writer's last handwritten draft.

September, October and November
are not mentioned in any of
Shakespeare's works.

The only burp in Shakespeare
is by Sir Toby Belch.

A large fart
has about the same volume
as a can of fizzy drink.

Champagne bubbles
are basically
yeast farts.

Carp can live without
oxygen for months.

Fish eaten by
jellyfish cost South Korea
up to $200 million a year
in lost revenue.

225 Canadian fishermen
die every year while
urinating over the
side of their boat.

400,000 people
died building the
Great Wall of China.

The Roman emperor Domitian
held a death-themed dinner party
with black plates, charred food and
conversations about murder
and sudden death.

A French workman's café
was accidentally awarded
a Michelin star in 2017 after a
mix up with a Parisian restaurant
of the same name.

Salvador Dalí went
to restaurants with his
pet ocelot, claiming it
was a cat with a pattern
painted on.

Penguins'
adult offspring return home
and demand to be fed.

7% of American adults
believe that chocolate milk
comes from brown cows.

Prince Philip was born
on a kitchen table
in Corfu.

Hawaii
gets bigger by
165 square metres
every day.

All the world's beaches
lined up in a row
would reach
the Moon.

A grain of sand
officially measures
between 0.06 and 2
millimetres across.

The world
is running out
of sand.

All 436,800 sandwiches
sold on the streets of London in 1851
were ham sandwiches.

'Sweet sizzlin' green beans' are
35% more likely to be ordered than
'Healthy energy-boosting green beans',
even if prepared in the same way.

Hungry female praying mantises
pretend to be interested in sex
and then eat any interested
males who turn up.

Army cutworm moths
are 70% fat.

A pair of the
world's largest butterflies
sell for $10,000 on
the black market.

Butterflies
use their tongues
like drinking straws.

A woodpecker's tongue
is coiled around
its brain.

Seeds
have brains
that tell them when
to sprout.

Tumbleweeds
are native to Russia,
not the US.

The world's
leading cannabis expert
has never smoked
a joint.

No human beings
have ever had
sex in space.

Giraffes
have blue tongues,
and nobody knows why.

There is a
Guinness World Record
for 'most matchsticks extinguished
with the tongue'.

The longest
single jump by a bullfrog
was 4 feet 3 inches.

Polka-dot tree frogs
are fluorescent.

Half the wild boars
in the Czech Republic
are radioactive.

Mouse livers
grow 40% larger
at night.

40% of elephants
in captivity are
obese.

Elephants
disperse seeds
up to 40 miles away.

There is only one
documented case of
an elephant giving birth
to triplets.

Twins
live longer than
non-twins.

Identical twins
live longer than
non-identical twins.

Identical
male twins
live longer than
identical female twins.

Identical twins
don't run in
families.

The royal family
uses the word 'smart'
instead of 'posh'.

'Posh' boys' names
suggested by *Tatler*
include Barclay, Mao, Uxorious
and Npeter (the 'N' is silent).

'Posh' girls' names
suggested by *Tatler*
include Czar-Czar, Estonia,
Hum and Figgy.

When the BBC remade
Swallows and Amazons in 2016,
Titty was renamed Tatty.

The first English librarian
was named Edward Edwards.

The spokesman for the
British Leafy Salads Association
is called Dieter Lloyd.

The director of dance
at the Paris Opera Ballet
from 2014 to 2016 was
Benjamin Millepied.

The US
presidential limo
is called 'The Beast'.

The wife of
US President Lyndon B. Johnson
had a brother called
Thomas Jefferson.

LBJ's wife's name was 'Bird';
when she became First Lady,
she was known as
Lady Bird.

A group of ladybirds
is called a 'loveliness'.

Ladybirds
bleed poison
when threatened.

To make themselves
appear more threatening,
western spotted skunks
do handstands.

The surname Smellie
has become 71% less common
since 1881.

The bird-dung crab spider
looks and smells like dung
and eats flies that are
attracted to it.

A *smell-feast*
is someone who
shows up to a party
just for the food.

The word 'rooster'
was coined so Americans
didn't have to use
the word 'cock'.

Cockerels
lure hens for sex
by pretending to have
found food.

Female market squid
display fake testicles to avoid
the advances of males.

Female deep-sea squid
store sperm in
their arms.

Squid can edit
their own brain genes.

You can predict the winner
of a fight between two octopuses
by looking at their colours.

Female blanket octopuses are
10,000 times heavier
than the males.

All octopuses
are venomous but
only the blue-ringed octopus
is harmful to humans.

Seattle Aquarium
holds a Valentine's event
where you can watch
octopuses mating.

Visiting an aquarium can
lower your blood pressure.

The mouth of the blue whale at
Gothenburg's Natural History Museum
used to have a café in it.

Whales communicate by
jumping out of the water and
splashing on the surface.

Killer whales
can learn to speak
dolphin.

English speakers
can learn French in
half the time it takes to
learn Welsh.

The world's largest
Spanish-speaking country
is Mexico.

More than 350 languages
are spoken in Mexico,
as well as Spanish.

In the Spanish version
of *Terminator 2*, Arnie says
'*Sayonara*, baby' rather than
'*Hasta la vista*, baby'.

In the Japanese version
of *Terminator 2*, Arnie says
'Cheerio, love'.

Before *Star Trek*,
William Shatner starred in
Incubus, where the
dialogue was all
in Esperanto.

William Shatner insisted
a *Star Trek* script be rewritten
so that Kirk, rather than Spock, had
the first interracial kiss on TV.

There have been no weddings
in St Hilda's Church in Yorkshire
for 12 years because of
a bat infestation.

Bats contain more viruses
that are dangerous to humans
than any other species.

In medieval Germany,
it was thought that wearing
the left eye of a bat as a talisman
would make you invisible.

NASA
invented
invisible braces.

According to
state law in New Mexico,
Pluto is still
a planet.

The global
beauty and anti-ageing
industry is worth
$999 billion
a year.

Ostrich feathers
were once worth
as much as
diamonds.

Fossilised excrement
is worth more if it has
'the classic poo look'.

Sloths excrete
only once
a week.

Polar bears
can smell seals
40 miles away.

The smell of
rosemary improves
children's memories.

Hyperthymesia
is the inability to ever
forget anything.

Cryptomnesia is
when a memory floats
into your conscious mind
and you mistake it for
an original idea.

Harry Beck
designed the iconic
London Underground map
for a one-off fee of 10 guineas.

90% of
London Underground stations
are north of the Thames.

Tube trains
are cleaned with
magnetic wands.

Mars has
no magnetic
field.

All Dutch trains
run on wind energy.

California
generates almost half
the solar energy
in the US.

Almond orchards
use 10% of the water
in California.

Texas has
over 1,300 different
kinds of soil.

The average British garden
contains over 20,000
slugs and snails.

Half of British gardeners
cannot name a
single shrub.

Plants can
tell the time
better than people.

Trees have
their own
songs.

The father
of Paul Dacre,
editor of the *Daily Mail*,
wrote songs for
Bing Crosby.

Adam Ant's mum
was Paul McCartney's
cleaner.

Surgeons often
operate to
music.

Richard III was
a blue-eyed blond.

William IV's head
was shaped like
a pineapple.

George III
didn't see the sea
till he was 34 years old.

Prince Charles
has waited longer to
become king than any
heir to the throne in
British history.

Human DNA begins
to degenerate at
55 years old.

DNA testing
is mandatory
in Kuwait.

If all the data from
all of human history
were encoded onto DNA,
it would fit into a container
the size and weight of
two pickup trucks.

Data has
overtaken oil as the
world's most valuable
resource.

India is
the world's largest
exporter of beef.

The Department of Medals
at India's Ministry of Defence
doesn't make any medals,
it just buys them
at the market.

The UK's Ministry of Defence
owns three and a half times as
many pieces of fine art as it does
warships, tanks, helicopters,
planes and submarines.

Ethiopia has
a space programme.

Iceland
imports ice cubes.

Australia
moves 2.7 inches
a year.

No one is
ever born in
Vatican City.

Venus Williams
has spent more than
a year of her life
at Wimbledon.

The word 'queue'
is the only word in English
that sounds the same if you
remove four of its letters.

On average, people will wait
six minutes in a queue
before giving up.

People are reluctant to join
a queue of more than
six people.

The halfway line at
Brazil's Zerão football stadium
runs exactly along
the equator.

David Beckham
owns over 1,000 pairs
of football boots.

To cover Gareth Bale's salary,
Real Madrid need to sell 1.2 million
football shirts per year.

American football teams can have
up to six captains, but only one
gets to call the coin toss.

Argentinian footballer
Carlos Tevez earns
£1 a second.

Kendo masters
get paid nothing.

Elephant polo
is popular in India, Nepal
and Thailand.

In Thailand,
it is illegal to
own more than 120
playing cards.

There are
only 70 wolves
in Norway.

The Viking King
Olaf Tryggvason could jog
round the outside of his longship
on its oars while it was
being rowed.

Iceland's elite police
counter-terrorism unit
is known as the
Viking Squad.

Firing squad
is a legal method
of execution in
Oklahoma.

The most murderous
mammals are
meerkats.

Cats have whiskers on
their front paws as
well as their
faces.

Seals have
retractable nipples.

Wolves have
a sense of fair play.

Dolphins have
no vocal cords.

Cockroaches
have no
ears.

Orang-utans
are good at
charades.

A group
of opossums is
called a 'grin'.

Bumblebees
can learn to
play golf.

Ancient beekeepers
took their beehives on hikes
if there weren't enough
flowers near by.

Bumblebees
can make a flower open by
buzzing in middle C.

Male bees
sometimes chase
aeroplanes in mistake
for female bees.

Oslo has
a 'bee highway'
that is planted with flowers
and winds through
the city.

Norway has
a 'tooth bank'
which is aiming to collect
100,000 milk teeth.

The Mayans
drilled holes in their teeth
to fit precious stones in.

40% of toothbrushes
have red handles.

When Winston Churchill
got really angry, he would throw
his teeth across the room.

Winston Churchill
believed in aliens.

After investigation,
only 1.8% of UFOs remain
'unidentified'.

The first British plan
to put a man on the Moon
was made by Oliver Cromwell's
brother-in-law.

Comet West
appeared in 1976;
its previous visit took place
before humans existed, and it will
return in 250,000 years.

Cosmic dust
left over from the
dawn of time has been
found on rooftops
in Paris.

Since 1993,
the Hubble Space Telescope
has been the source for 25% of
all published astronomy papers.

In 1900,
France built a telescope
which was so long it couldn't
be pointed at the sky.

The Ottoman Empire
was so large that it takes
21 countries to cover
the area today.

In the Ottoman Empire,
anyone who took the throne would
kill all his brothers to stop them
assassinating him.

Kookaburras
have a hook in their top beak
which is specifically designed for
murdering their siblings.

The most
destructive predator
in New Zealand
is the possum.

Dragonflies
have a kill rate
of 95%.

Dragonflies
can see directly
behind themselves.

The purple sea urchin's body
acts as one giant eye.

Sulfhemoglobinemia is
a condition where a person
develops green blood.

There's a set of
German traffic lights
that have been on red
for 30 years.

Preference
for the colour yellow
declines with age.

Yellow cars
are the least likely to
have an accident.

The toy case
in a Kinder Surprise
is yellow to represent
an egg yolk.

An Essex egg farmer
massively increased his output
by playing Radio 2 to his hens
for 15 hours a day.

Test tube babies
thrive if played techno music
24 hours a day.

Illegal baby names
in New Zealand include
Lucifer, Christ and Messiah.

54% of Americans
believe science conflicts
with religion, but not
with their own.

Aristotle thought
plants had
souls.

On 4 April 2017,
there were 335,765,099
different products available
on Amazon.

40% of pages
in LEGO catalogues
contain some kind
of violence.

LEGO
is part-owner of the
world's largest wind turbine.

Wind turbines
were invented almost
150 years ago.

⌈ 250 ⌉

The word 'soon'
used to mean
'right now'.

The Yorkshire greeting 'eh up'
was originally used
by Vikings.

Vladimir Nabokov
used the word 'mauve'
44 times more often than
it usually appears in English.

The *Oxford English Dictionary*
was originally offered
to Cambridge.

King's College, Cambridge,
has won more Nobel Prizes
than France.

Italy has more
bank robberies than
the rest of Europe combined.

The king of Rwanda
lives in a terraced house
in Manchester.

Sir James Dyson
owns more English farmland
than the Queen.

Britons use
the winking emoji
twice as often as any
other nationality.

There are emojis
for 'asshat', 'douchebag'
and 'cockwomble'.

The dung piles
of white rhinos are
their social network,
telling other rhinos
how they are.

Scientists can tell
how old you are from
the fingerprint smudges
on your phone.

Humans have
adapted the way they walk
so they can look at
their phones.

'What is my IP?'
is the most common
search on Google.

Every month,
as many people google
'How to make slime'
as 'How to make
love'.

In Wisconsin,
the word people
most often google
'how to spell' is
'Wisconsin'.

The most misspelled word
in New Mexico
is 'banana'.

The first monkey
known to have got drunk
was reported in 1779 by
the ship's doctor on
HMS *Dorchester*.

Dogs prefer humans
who are kind to
other humans.

Most dogs
prefer praise
to food.

98% of Britons
consider themselves to be
among the nicest 50%
of the population.

Violent criminals
rate themselves more moral,
kind, self-controlled and honest
than the average person.

In 1880s gangland New York,
having someone punched cost $2,
but there was a $15 charge for
chewing their ear off.

A million dollars
in used $10 notes would
come with a bonus of
1.17 cents' worth
of cocaine.

The International Olympic Committee
declared the 1980 Moscow Olympics
'the first drug-free Olympics'.

For the Rio Olympics,
70,000 families were displaced.

The average Olympic Games
goes 156% over
its budget.

The 1976 Montreal Olympics
overspent its budget
by 720%.

The average person spends
375 days in a lifetime
folding laundry.

Only 10% of
homes in India have a
washing machine.

The sandals of the
Pueblo people of New Mexico
had enough space
for six toes.

There is a Danish myth
that you can get drunk by
soaking your feet
in vodka.

After migration,
birds overeat and
stagger around,
'drunk' on food.

In 2013,
American competitive eater
Joey Chestnut ate 141 eggs
in eight minutes.

Guinness dropped
speed-eating records
in 1991.

The record number of people
dressed like Einstein
in one place
is 404.

The mathematics that
makes Wi-Fi possible was
developed by a team of physicists
looking for tiny black holes.

Nobody knows
how many holes there are
in the human body. Most of them
are for sweat ducts and
hair follicles.

1 in 100 Britons
are born with a tiny hole
in the top of their
ears.

People who use
Google Glass spectacles
are known as
Glassholes.

Head lice lay eggs
to match your
hair colour.

The mola fish
lays 300 million eggs
but only two of them
will make it to
adulthood.

Italy produces 44,000
tonnes of snails a year.
Their eggs are sold as caviar
and their mucus is used
in skin creams.

The human body produces
a gallon of mucus
a day.

Tuna are
more closely related
to humans than
to sharks.

Every winter,
great white sharks
swim for 40 days to meet up
between Mexico and Hawaii,
and nobody knows why.

Sharks
are older than
trees.

Older fish
live longer if
fed the faeces of
younger fish.

Smelts
are fish that
smell of cucumber.

Sea cucumbers
fire their gonads
out of their bodies
to distract predators.

The polyclad flatworm
has multiple anuses
on its back.

Some face mites
can't excrete, so they
eat until they
explode.

The McDonald's Filet-O-Fish
was invented for Catholics who
couldn't eat meat
on Fridays.

During Lent,
fasting is suspended
on Sundays.

Tarantulas
can last two years
between meals.

The British Tarantula Society
was founded by
Ann Webb.

The finance director
of QuidditchUK is called
Megan Snape.

British Telecom,
Prozac and Hobnobs were
all named by the same man.

The chocolate
on a Hobnob is on
the bottom of the biscuit,
not the top.

60% of people
eating chocolate rabbits
bite the ears off first.

Oligophagous
means 'eating only a few
types of food'.

Omnicompetent
means 'able to deal
with anything'.

Onomatomania
is the frustration at
not being able to think of
the right word.

Oorie is
a Scots word meaning
'miserable in cold weather'.

'Marmite'
comes from
an old French word
meaning 'hypocritical'.

Only 1% of people
who buy marmalade are
under the age of 28.

The tea genome is
four times longer than
the coffee genome.

Since 1945,
all tanks in the British army
have been equipped
with tea-making
facilities.

Hominids
have used fire
for 500,000 years,
but only learned to make it
12,000 years ago.

Drug lord Pablo Escobar
once burned $2 million in cash
in one night to keep his
family warm.

Pablo Escobar
offered to pay the
whole of Colombia's
national debt.

Iceland has
a bar called
Pablo Discobar.

Arda Turan,
the Turkish midfielder
who plays for Barcelona,
pays the electricity bills
for everyone living in
his old block of flats
in Istanbul.

The energy used in the world
at any one time is enough to run
10 billion 100-watt
lightbulbs.

Ta'ū island
in American Samoa
runs on 100% solar energy.

Ancient Roman baths
were often warmed
with solar power.

Until the 5th century,
the must-have Roman gadget
was a portable sundial.

The Romans
raised birds for food in
special aviaries and fed them figs
that were pre-chewed
by the staff.

Ancient Romans painted
extra doors opposite real doors
to make rooms look bigger.

A *ka* door
was a fake door built
in Egyptian tombs as a link
between the living and the dead.

The Nuba people of Sudan
have keyhole-shaped doorways
to make room for the
wide loads carried
on their heads.

The 'doorway effect' is
when you walk into a room
and completely forget
what you came in for.

Climbing a tree
can help you to
remember
things.

Trees
can recognise
their offspring.

You can
attract an emu by
waving a handkerchief at it.

An *emuu* was
the original mother of
each animal and plant species
in ancient Finland.

In Finnish folklore,
the first person to use a sauna
will become its 'sauna elf'
when they die.

Finland has
three million saunas
for a population of
5.5 million
people.

To one decimal place,
the population of Greenland
per square mile is
officially
0.0.

Canada has
underground water
that is two billion years old.

Pure water
is very slightly sour.

It takes 52 litres of water
to make a cup of tea
with milk and
two sugars.

The first 'chaser'
was alcohol taken to
remove the aftertaste
of coffee.

The coffee berry borer
is the only animal that
lives exclusively on
coffee beans.

Mary Berry
has never ordered
a pizza.

The world's first illustrated cookbook
included a recipe for pizza
topped with sugar
and rose water.

Rose-tinted spectacles
for chickens were used by
US farmers in the early 1900s.

According to
a study in Ethiopia,
you can avoid catching malaria
by carrying a chicken
at all times.

In the late 1980s,
officials in India released
25,000 turtles into the Ganges
to eat dead bodies.

The first gentlemen's club in America
was formed for the purpose of
eating turtle soup.

A hamster
that eats nothing but corn
will turn into a crazed
cannibal.

The favourite food
of Adélie penguins is
jellyfish genitals.

Egyptian vultures
get their vibrant yellow beaks
from eating yellow
cow dung.

In the 18th century,
a St Kilda islander would
eat up to 18 seabirds a day.

The Orkney Islands
are as close to Norway
as they are to Aberdeen.

The world's shortest scheduled flight,
between two islands in the Orkneys,
takes as little as 53 seconds.

The world's shortest international flight,
over Lake Constance between
Austria and Switzerland,
takes eight minutes.

Using a leaf blower for
half an hour creates more emissions
than driving a pickup truck
3,800 miles.

In 2016,
for the first time ever,
more electricity was produced
in the UK by wind than by coal.

In 1888,
hailstones as
big as oranges
fell in India.

Orange cars
hold their value better
than cars of any
other colour.

Sean Connery
was once caught speeding by
a policeman called Sergeant
James Bond.

Fidel Castro
helped edit the novels of
Gabriel García Márquez.

In Jamaica,
Clarks shoes are
a must-have gangsta
fashion accessory.

In 17th-century London,
women wore high-heeled clogs.

Macrophiles are
men who fantasise
about sex with
giant women.

The Statue of Liberty
has a 35-foot
waistline.

If a Formula One driver
puts on 11 lb in weight,
it can add 0.2 seconds
to their lap time.

Ron Hill,
the first Briton to
win the Boston Marathon,
ran every day for 19,032 days
from December 1964
to January 2017.

Australia's first Olympian
ran the marathon, then
became delirious and
punched a spectator.

After the first official
women's boxing match in the UK,
the press stormed the ring and it
collapsed under their weight.

At the launch of the
first ballpoint pen in the US,
the crowds had to be restrained
by riot police.

The first edition of
Wisden Cricketers' Almanack was
112 pages long and padded out
with accounts of the trial of
King Charles I.

The first animal to be
ejected from a supersonic jet
with a parachute
was a bear.

In 18th-century France,
fashionable women
styled their hair
à la rhinocéros.

Tiaras
were originally worn
by men.

1,000 years ago,
shirts and skirts were
the same thing.

Men are
six times more likely
to be struck by lightning
than women.

The odds that
Tasmanian tigers still exist
have been calculated as
1.6 trillion to one.

Some villages in the
Central African Republic
allow lions to live near by so
locals can steal their kill.

A 19th-century way
to prevent toothache
was to tie a dead mole
around your neck.

In 2016,
a 155-year-old mousetrap,
kept as an exhibit in a
Berkshire museum,
caught a mouse.

There are
1,111 museums in
Switzerland.

James Franco's
Museum of Non-Visible Art
contains no physical work, just ideas.
A 'piece' called *Fresh Air* sold for
$10,000.

Germany has a
Museum of Snoring.

Jet-lagged hamsters
should be given
Viagra.

Tampon
is French for
'rubber stamp'.

The Symptoms, Nature,
Cause, and Cure of a Gonorrhoea
was published in 1818 by
William Cockburn.

Condoms are
used by car mechanics
to mend punctures.

People who
buy 'bags for life' are
safer drivers.

More than
200 drivers in Britain
are at least 100 years old.

During the First World War,
1,000 double-decker London buses,
complete with drivers and mechanics,
were sent to the front line.

Bus horns in Indonesia
play tunes, are sampled by DJs
and are available
as apps.

The 23A bus
from Salisbury Plain to Imber runs
only once a year.

Only one
blind person
has climbed Everest.

Cold elephants
are kept warm by
villagers in India knitting
jumpers for them.

The traditional Indian way
of sobering up a drunk elephant
was to feed it three pounds
of melted butter.

Dairy cows
in Norway must have
a mattress to
lie down on.

The Boston Public Library
has a 'car wash'
for books.

181 books published in 2016
had the F-word in their title,
compared with just
52 in 2015.

There is a
German airline that allows
an extra free kilo of hand luggage,
provided it's books.

There is a bookshop
in Shanghai that
sells books by
the kilo.

Armageddon
is a real place in Israel.

There's a town in India
called Poo.

Nothing, Arizona,
has a population
of none.

By 2030,
there will be no glaciers
in Glacier Mountain Park,
Montana.

Macedonia
has more mountain peaks
than any country
in the world.

Brazil's
highest mountain
was unknown until the 1950s
because it is permanently
shrouded in cloud.

Asperitas is
a cloud formation
that resembles an
unmade bedsheet.

Each sheet of
parchment used to record
British Acts of Parliament
costs £35.

Britain's
tallest waterfall is
twice as high as Niagara
but entirely underground.

There is a point
in the Pacific Ocean where,
if you drilled directly down
through the planet, you would
arrive back in the
Pacific Ocean.

A whole chapter of *Moby Dick*
is dedicated to the fact
that whales don't
have noses.

The main danger
dolphins face underwater
is drowning.

Three-quarters of Americans
are in debt when
they die.

Only a quarter
of British adults eat
their five a day.

Golden Delicious apples
have almost three times
as many genes as
people.

Oregano
is a name used for
a dozen different plants.

The fastest-growing plant
is bamboo, which grows
at three centimetres
an hour.

The slowest-growing plant
is a moss that grows less than
1 millimetre a year.

Plants can tell when
one of their leaves is being eaten,
and react to try to stop it.

There are four times
as many species of orchid
as there are species
of mammal.

Camels
gave humans
the common cold.

Zebras
can be scanned
like barcodes.

Science
knows more about
coffee, wine and tomatoes than
it does about breast milk.

Scientists
can predict when
an elderly person is going to fall over
three weeks before it happens.

Obdormition is
when your arm falls asleep
from lying on it.

Oniomania
is the compulsive urge
to buy things, including
(but not necessarily)
onions.

Obscurum per obscurious
is an explanation more complicated
than the thing it's trying
to explain.

Obsidional
means boring people by
staying too long.

Salvador Dalí's moustache
was set at ten past ten,
like the hands
of a clock.

9 out of 10
hedge funds are a
waste of time
and money.

At New Year in Brazil,
people eat lentils because
they symbolise money.

Andrew Jackson,
the face on the US $20 bill,
was opposed to paper currency.

Warren Buffett has
been paying income tax
since he was 14.

In 2016,
a worker at the
Royal Canadian Mint
was caught smuggling
gold coins out in
his bottom.

Airlines make more money
selling air miles
than seats.

£1.5 million in cash
has been eaten by British pets
since 2003.

The world's largest pet rabbit
is 4 feet 4 inches long, weighs 3½ stone
and eats 4,000 carrots a year.

The world's largest volcano is
1,000 miles from Japan
under the sea.

A volcano
in Guatemala has
erupted once an hour for
the last 94 years.

If you stood on top of
a mountain on the Moon
and fired a gun at the horizon,
you could shoot yourself
in the back.

More people in America
own more than 10 guns than
there are people in the
whole of Denmark.

In the US,
offal is known as
'variety meats'.

Serbia is
home to the
World Testicle Cooking Championships.

Britain exports
deer testicles
to China.

Sigmund Freud
spent a month in 1876
searching for eels' testicles,
but never found any.

Eels that swim
3,000 miles across the Atlantic
lose weight from
their bones.

The gulper eel
has a mouth which is bigger
than the rest of its body.

The breadcrumb sponge
has been 'discovered' so many times
it has 56 different names.

A fifth of all
known species of coral
were named by the same man.

The number of
marine species is unknown;
estimates range from one million
to 10 million.

Every spring,
thousands of firefly squid
light up Toyama Bay, Japan,
glimmering like stars
in the water.

The world's oldest fish,
Grandad, died in 2017
in his mid-nineties.

People
who read books
live longer than people
who don't.

In the 17th century,
blood from the recently deceased
was used to treat
epilepsy.

Aspirin
confused people at first.
One headache sufferer
strapped a tablet
to his head.

Botox
was developed
to treat double vision.

Aardvarks' eyes
don't reflect light
in the dark.

Charlotte Brontë
could see in the dark
well enough
to read.

John Dollond
of Dollond & Aitchison
invented glasses for
horses.

There is a Chinese
brand of spectacles called
Helen Keller.

There are four cases
of blind people regaining their sight
after tripping over the leads
of their guide dogs.

The popularity
of dog breeds is
less influenced by breed,
appearance or temperament
than by their appearance in films.

J. R. R. Tolkien and C. S. Lewis
went to the cinema together to see
Snow White and the Seven Dwarfs
but didn't enjoy it.

John Williams
has never seen any
of the *Star Wars* movies
he composed the music for.

Chuck Berry
had a degree in
hairdressing.

Roman women
donated their hair for use as
military catapult elastic.

Trap-jaw ants can
close their jaws with such force
they catapult themselves
through the air.

Manatees
adjust their buoyancy
through controlled flatulence.

Walruses
use birds as toys.

40% of toys
in Russia are bought
by grandparents.

1 in 5
children's building sets
and action figures in the UK
are bought by adults
for their own use.

Sex toys in
Japan were known as
'laughter devices'.

North Korea's
entire Internet has
only 28 websites.

70% of online ads
are never seen
by humans.

'Wi-Fi'
isn't short
for anything.

It takes
65 milliseconds
for a message to cross
the Atlantic.

Tidsoptimist is a
Danish word for someone who
thinks they have more
time than they
actually do.

Shturmovschina
is Russian for working
frantically to meet a deadline,
having not done anything
for the last month.

'To egrote' is
to pretend to be ill
to avoid work.

A *lychnobite* is
someone who sleeps all day
and works all night.

‘Hit the farter’
is Australian slang
for ‘go to bed’.

‘Bumpsy’ is
17th-century slang for
‘drunk’.

‘Hot beef’ was
Victorian rhyming slang
for ‘Stop thief’.

The use of
CAPITAL LETTERS
TO DENOTE SHOUTING
dates back to the
19th century.

If you shout
at the Taj Mahal,
it takes 28 seconds for the
echoes to fade away.

Inscriptions discovered
under Peterborough Cathedral suggest
it may be 1,000 years older than
previously thought.

Covering buildings
with olive oil protects them
against acid rain.

Olive Oyl
appeared 10 years
before Popeye.

People
eating popcorn
remember adverts less.

Americans spend
more than a year of their life
flipping channels.

There are more
CCTV cameras in Hackney
than in the whole
of Wales.

In Montenegro,
Only Fools and Horses
is called
Mucke.

The average
BBC viewer is
over 60 years old.

At 104 years old,
Jack Reynolds became the
oldest person to get a tattoo,
and, at 105, the oldest to
ride a roller coaster.

Riding a roller coaster
can help patients to expel
their kidney stones.

Liu Bang,
founder of the Chinese Han dynasty,
hated Confucians so much that
whenever he saw one he
would urinate
into his hat.

Ostriches
are the only birds
with a bladder.

Electronic devices are
scrambling the navigational cues
used by migrating birds.

Tens of millions of birds
have been ringed by ornithologists,
but only 2.2% of them have
ever been seen again.

The world record
for the most bird species
seen by one person in a year
is 6,841.

Giant
flying turkeys
as big as kangaroos
once roamed Australia.

A 'willy-willy'
is a tiny tornado found
in the Australian outback.

Australian
compass termites
build their mounds on a
north–south axis.

Startled deer run
due north or due south
so they don't crash
into each other.

The highest point in Mauritania
cannot be found with
a compass due to
magnetic rocks.

The US Embassy
in Kathmandu has
guidelines on what to do
if a yeti is found.

One contender for the
geographical centre of America
is a place called Center.

Didcot, Oxfordshire,
is officially the most
normal town
in Britain.

Four times
as many ferrets live
in the south-east of England
as in Yorkshire.

1 in 8
young Britons have
never seen a cow
in real life.

England is
smaller than
New York state.

Kansas is only
the seventh-flattest
state in the US.

50% of US territory
is under the sea.

85% of Vakkaru Island
in the Maldives
is made up of
fish faeces.

Three-quarters
of all ocean creatures
glow in the dark.

The bottom
of the sea is
surprisingly noisy.

Samba music
makes curry taste
10% spicier.

The best-selling British music act
in America in the 1990s
was The Beatles.

Lithuania
has a memorial
to Frank Zappa, even though
he never went to
Lithuania.

Lou Reed
once played a gig
just for dogs.

Fidel Castro's
favourite cow had its
own food taster.

Cuba
bans statues
of living Cubans.

An effigy of the Pope
stuffed with live cats was
burned at the coronation of
Elizabeth I.

Avocado toast
is poisonous
to lemurs.

To catch a rabbit,
a stoat will hypnotise it with
thrashing dance moves.

Female dragonflies
fake death to avoid
sex with males.

Seahorses
greet their partners
with a dance
every day.

Horseshoe crab
blood costs up to
$28,000 a pint.

420,000 people die
in the world each year
as a result of
falling.

Rottweilers
are used in Norway for
mountain rescue.

Louisiana only
banned cockfighting
in 2008.

In 2016,
a llama-dressing-up
contest in Minnesota
was won by an
alpaca.

When dinosaurs
roamed the Earth,
days were only 23 hours long.

Until three million years ago,
whales were less than
30 feet long.

The largest-ever photo
was 111 feet wide and taken
with a pinhole camera
three storeys high.

The cuckoo in the
world's largest cuckoo clock
weighs 23½ stone.

In 2017,
there were three times
as many robins in Britain
as there were
in 1987.

An Arctic tern
weighs about the same
as a bar of soap.

The world's smallest fox
is only 10 times larger than
the world's largest ant.

Racing ferrets
sometimes fall asleep
halfway along the course.

More than
200 US colleges offer courses
in paranormal phenomena.

90% of students
have hallucinated that
their phone is buzzing
in their pocket.

Nokia
didn't make phones
from 2011 to 2016.

Self-driving cars
play *Grand Theft Auto*
to learn how to
drive better.

Robots
cannot be taught
to lace a pair of
trainers.

The record for
the most Wimbledon titles
is held by Professor Bernard Neal:
he was croquet champion
38 times.

You can improve your darts game
by training yourself to dream
about playing darts.

Anemones have
slapping contests.

To tiny ocean creatures,
water is as thick
as jelly.

The California
black sea hare is
a giant slug
as big as
a cat.

The longest pet cat
in the world weighs 31 lb
and eats raw kangaroo meat.

There is no evidence that dogs
have a better sense of
smell than humans.

770 lb of dog hairs
are swept up after
Crufts each year.

American cocker spaniels
are all descended from
a single English dog
named Obo II.

William III of England,
Alexander III of Scotland,
Leopold V of Austria and
Louis IV of France all
died after falling
off a horse.

People put on a horse that is
too difficult for them to ride
are said to have been
'over-horsed'.

Bargibant's pygmy seahorses
are the size of a
50p coin.

A zeptosecond
(a trillionth of a billionth
of a second) is the smallest
unit of time ever
recorded.

Because it cannot be seen,
the Aymara people of the Andes
think of the future as
behind them.

In South America,
an ocelot is a *manigordo*,
or 'fat hands', because its
forepaws are much bigger
than its hind ones.

The Asian flat-headed cat
has webbed feet and
washes its prey
in water.

Cat videos
on YouTube are
not as popular as
dog videos.

The first pet cat
lived in Egypt
10,000 years
ago.

Between 1977 and 1998,
23 people in the US
caught the plague
from pet cats.

Rats who have sex
at least once a day for 14 days
grow more neurons
in their brain.

In the mating season,
mouse lemur testes swell
to become bigger than
their brains.

Snails use
just two brain cells
to decide if they're hungry.

Giant pandas
born in the US
prefer American food
and understand English
better than Chinese.

China buys
bottled fresh air
from Britain.

There are
600,000 psychopaths
in Britain.

The BBC's weekly
global audience
is 372 million
people.

The best people
at making lists of
random numbers are
25-year-olds.

Fāl-gūsh,
or eavesdropping
on random strangers,
is a method of divination
practised in Iran.

Ololygmancy
is predicting the future
by interpreting the
howling of dogs.

Psithurism
is the sound
of rustling leaves.

53 million years ago,
Antarctica was covered
in palm trees.

Only one
female film director
has ever won the
Palme d'Or.

Rapper
Tupac Shakur
was a former ballet dancer.

Cary Grant
started his career
as an acrobat.

There are only
16 circus animals
left in the UK.

The Parliament of Bats
was held in Leicester
in 1426.

Redditch
once made 90%
of the world's needles.

The only wooden stocks
in Oxfordshire are
in Woodstock.

26% of Britons
own their homes,
compared with 75% of Poles.

For the first time in over a century,
18- to 34-year-old Britons are
less likely to live with a
spouse than with
their parents.

The parents
of most geniuses
aren't geniuses.

Orang-utan mothers
breastfeed for
eight years.

The world's eight richest men
are worth more than
half the population
of the world
combined.

Most people who were
dollar billionaires in 1995
aren't billionaires today.

Only 11 of the
1,810 billionaires
in the world
are black.

The most expensive jeans
in the world cost
$10,000.

Neanderthals
wore capes.

Renaissance women
removed their body hair
with arsenic.

Ancient Egypt
had nine-pin bowling.

Martin Luther
had his own bowling lane.

An Adamite
is someone who
walks around naked for
religious reasons.

Shivviness is
an old Yorkshire word for
the uncomfortable feeling you get
from wearing new underwear.

Kalsarikannit
is the Finnish for
drinking at home alone
in your underpants.

A *deipnosophist* is
someone who is good at
small talk.

When introduced to a stranger,
Argentinians stand closest
and Romanians
furthest away.

Members of the
Nigerian parliament earn
10,000 times the national
minimum wage.

The 9th US president,
William Henry Harrison,
claimed he was born in a log cabin
but was actually born
in a mansion.

Orson Welles
wrote speeches for
Franklin D. Roosevelt.

Americans spend
$11 billion a year on
the pursuit of happiness.

People who
have children are
less happy but
live longer.

Cheerful women are
less likely to be
promoted.

The man who
popularised the
high five has only
four fingers.

Only six people
are qualified to raise or lower
Tower Bridge.

On his retirement,
the senior crayon-maker at Crayola
finally admitted he was
colour-blind.

All RSPCA inspectors
must be able to swim
50 metres fully clothed
in 2.5 minutes.

Billy Muir
from Orkney
has 20 jobs, including
lighthouse keeper, firefighter,
rubbish collector, electrician,
tour guide and builder.

Autocracies build
more skyscrapers than
democracies.

There are more than
20,000 abandoned villages
in Russia.

Citibank
employs more than 23,000
compliance officers.

There are more than
45,000 species
of spider.

There are 20,000
edible-cricket farms
in Thailand.

Gillette
stopped sponsoring cricket
after market research showed that
their brand was more associated
with sport than with razors.

Celebrities got more
mentions in British newspapers
than politicians for the
first time in 1901.

Trains first got more
newspaper mentions
than horses in 1902, and
football beat cricket
in 1920.

149–0 is the
world's highest football score.
The losers lost on purpose
and all the goals were
own goals.

While at AC Milan,
defender Paolo Maldini
averaged only one tackle
every other game.

Bossaball
is a kind of volleyball
played on trampolines
to music.

Rectangular
trampolines are
safer than round ones.

Socks in
international pro cycling
must be no higher than midway
between ankle and knee, and
it's someone's job to check.

At the 1968 Olympics,
Bob Beamon broke the world
long jump record by so much
they had to find another
tape measure.

There is no
standard height for
'sea level'.

Less than 1%
of Camemberts
are made to official
Camembert standards.

'Onion Johnnies' were
Frenchmen on bicycles
with berets and stripy tops
and strings of onions
round their necks.

Bermuda
celebrates New Year by
dropping a massive illuminated
papier mâché onion from
the town hall.

175 countries produce
an onion crop.

The ancient Greek poet Archestratus
described goose liver pâté as
'the soul of the goose'.

Bar-headed geese
can hyperventilate without
getting dizzy.

Blind people
can learn to see with
their tongues.

Frogs' tongues
are 10 times softer
than human tongues.

Frogs survived
the asteroid that
wiped out the dinosaurs.

The world's largest
dinosaur footprint is longer
than Mark Zuckerberg
is tall.

Prince's
flip-flops had
three-inch
heels.

The pressure per square inch
the Eiffel Tower puts on the ground
is about the same as that of
a woman in high heels.

60% of the
world's shoes are
made in China.

Piñatas were
invented in China.

More people work in
the tea industry in China
than live in the UK.

The heat in curries
comes from chillies brought to India
by the Portuguese in the
15th century.

The Aztecs
dabbed chilli sauce on
their arrowheads.

The heaviest chilli ever grown
was planted by a man
called Edward Curry.

Washing machines in India
have a special mode for dealing
with curry stains.

Croatia has
a 210-foot-long sea organ
which is 'played'
by the tide.

Spring tides occur all year round;
the name has nothing to do
with the seasons.

Ancient Japan
had 72 seasons,
lasting around
five days each.

In Japan,
you can take exams in
how to throw house parties.

'Cocktail party syndrome'
is a rare genetic disorder that
makes people extremely
friendly.

Friendship has
more influence on
longevity than exercise,
diet, heart problems
and smoking.

Nobody knows
why we say
'hmm'.

Nobody knows
how many people
live in Nigeria.

Nobody knows
how many organs
we have.

All the organs
of Enrique Iglesias
are on the opposite side
of his body to normal.

Andy Murray
has three kneecaps.

Billy Ocean
has three lungs.

There is actually only
one ocean in
the world.

There are
two Air Force Ones.

The average person makes
35,000 decisions
a day.

300,000 objects
a year are lost on the
London Underground.

The first man to use
an umbrella in London
was pelted with rubbish.

The London borough of Southwark
is rented from the Queen
for £11 a year.

It is illegal to enter
the Houses of Parliament
in a suit of armour.

Sir Edmund Hillary and
Lady Thatcher became
Knights of the Garter
on the same day.

Lord Salisbury
ran the British Empire with
52 civil servants.

For the first time in history,
more species are being
lost every year
than found.

Children
under three years old
cannot imagine
the future.

Adults think
about the future
three times as often
as the past.

Stephen Hawking
predicts the human race
has only 1,000 years
left on Earth.

Dick Whittington,
Lord Mayor of London,
died in
1423.

23 Thanks

This book would not have been possible without the help of our friends and colleagues at QI – Alex Bell, Rob Blake, Will Bowen, Edward Brooke-Hitching, Stevyn Colgan, Mat Coward, Alice Campbell Davis, Jenny Doughty, Ben Dupré, Chris Emerson, Mandy Fenton, Piers Fletcher, Lauren Gilbert, John Kelly, Harry Lloyd, John Mitchinson, Andrew Hunter Murray, Justin Pollard, Anna Ptaszynski, Dan Schreiber and Liz Townsend.

A very special thank you to our editor Laura Hassan and to Faber & Faber, who have been home to QI's books for over a decade.

Index

This is here to help you find your favourite bits.
Like the facts themselves, we've kept it as simple as we can.

ballet 333; balloons 99; ballot papers 97; ballpoint pens 90,
281; balls 186, 187; Balmoral 196; bamboo 293; bananas
255; bands 113; bank accounts 11; Bank of England 11; bank
loans 5; bank robberies 252; banks 201; bankruptcy 201;
bans 6, 147, 319, 321; barcodes 294; Barra 55; bars 268;
baseball 192; basketball courts 190; bassists 113; baths 269;
bats 141, 181, 225, 334; BBC 216, 312, 331; beaches 55, 209;
beach-stealing 54; beaks 246, 276; Bob Beamon 345; beards
32; bears 281; The Beast 217; The Beatles 318; beauty 154,
165, 226; beauty contests 137; beavers 204; Harry Beck 228;
David Beckham 62, 237; Victoria Beckham 62; beds 12, 309;
bee-fly 87; beef 234, 309; beer 13, 14, 17, 60, 136, 137; bees
42, 242; beetles 47, 48, 154; Beijing 98; Sir Toby Belch 205;
beliefs 67, 207, 244, 249; Alexander Graham Bell 124; John
Bercow 2; berets 346; Berkshire 283; Bermuda 346; Chuck
Berry 305; Mary Berry 149, 274; betting 144; Bible 72,
142; Big Macs 150; Big Mouth Billy Bass 196; bigamy 69;
billionaires 336; bills 269; bindings 199; birds 3, 34, 59,
259, 270, 306, 313; birdsong 59; birthdays 196; births 214,
235, 339; bites 159, 265; black 157, 207; black belts 86;
black holes 260; black market 211; blackcurrant squash
129; blackcurrants 150; bladders 186, 313; Tony Blair 119;
blindfolds 146; blindness 287, 304, 347; blinking 174, 175;
blood 140, 218, 247, 302, 320; Blood Falls 185; blood pressure
222; blood tests 69; blood vessels 81; blue 212; blue whales
222; boars 213; boats 144, 207; bodies 247, 260, 261, 352;
body hair 337; body odour 102; Bolivia 177; Usain Bolt 87;
bombs 27, 171; Sergeant James Bond 278; bone marrow 156;
bones 96, 300; bonsai 70; book signings 1; books 1, 26, 116,
117, 199, 288, 302; bookshops 288; borders 200; boredom
295; borrowing 117; bossaball 344; Boston 176, 280, 288;

Botox 302; bottoms 47, 297; Bouvet Island 200; bowling lanes 337; box jellyfish 105; boxing 281; boys 142, 216; braces 225; Tom Brady 177; Johannes Brahms 73; brains 73, 90, 91, 133, 211, 221, 330; Bramley apples 70; *Brandenburg Concertos* 161; brands 303, 343; brandy 29, 160; Brazil 8, 10, 44, 146, 236, 290, 296; Brazilian wax 109; bread 92, 93, 111; breadcrumb sponge 300; breakfasts 139; breast milk 294; breastfeeding 335; breasts 99; breath 111; breathing 96; breeding 95, 108, 179, 304, 327; breweries 17; *The Bridge on the River Kwai* 125; bridges 54; brightness 167; Bristol 129; Britain 3, 14, 17, 23, 31, 40, 45, 65, 67, 69, 84, 95, 107, 147, 196, 202, 278, 291, 299, 331, 343; British army 267; British Acts of Parliament 290; British Empire 355; British Leafy Salads Association 217; British Library 118; British Tarantula Society 264; British Telecom 265; Britishness 120; Britons 9, 11, 12, 25, 26, 67, 91, 95, 108, 113, 162, 178, 253, 256, 260, 280, 286, 292, 316, 335; Broadway 10; Charlotte Brontë 303; brooms 189; brothers 246; brothers-in-law 244; brown 208; Brussels 145; Brussels sprouts 173; bubbles 206; bubblewrap 189; Buckingham Palace 203; Buddha 101; budgets 257; Buenos Aires Zoo 71; buffaloes 148; Warren Buffett 297; builders 207, 341; building sets 306; buildings 310; Bulgaria 22; bullfrogs 213; bulls 135; bumblebees 241; bumping 86, 309; bunkers 168; buoyancy 305; bureaucrats 53; burglars 75; burns 8, 159; burps 205; buses 286; George H. W. Bush 1; business 19, 23; butchering 67; butter 173, 287; butterflies 211; buzzing 242, 324

cables 132; Julius Caesar 92; cafés 207, 222; Caffè Nero 54; cakes 93; California 160, 229; California black sea hare 326; call signs 55; Cambodia 6; Cambridge 251; camels 137,

294; Camemberts 345; David Cameron 170; camouflage
47, 103; Canada 131, 207, 273, 297; cancer 99, 100; candyfloss machines 81; cannabis 104, 153, 212; cannibals 276;
cannons 114, 148; canoeing 159; cans 206; cantatas 65; Eric
Cantona 187; capes 337; capital letters 309; captains 237;
captivity 95; car doors 148; car parks 189; cards 143; Mariah
Carey 158; Caribbean 33; caribou 148; carnivores 24, 46;
carp 206; carrots 298; carrying 158, 271, 275; cars 37, 40,
65, 123, 248, 278, 285; carts 127; carving 192; cases 248;
cash 268, 297; Fidel Castro 50, 279, 319; cat lovers and haters
128; catalogues 250; catapults 305; caterpillars 48, 194;
Catholics 264; cats 2, 40, 128, 129, 203, 204, 208, 240, 319,
326, 329; cauldrons 150; cavalry officers 196; cavalry swords
172; caviar 261; CCTV 311; CDs 113; Robert Cecil 171;
celebrities 343; centenarians 91; Center 315; centipedes 194;
Central African Republic 283; CEOs 19; CERN 79; chairs
77; chameleons 47; champagne 172, 206; channel-flipping
311; chapattis 20; charades 241; Prince Charles 41, 232;
Charles I 281; chasers 274; checking 345; cheerfulness 340;
cheese 5; chefs 150; chess 143; chests 100; chewing 130, 256,
270; chickens 275; children 31, 32, 67, 68, 91, 95, 227, 306,
340; Chile 104; chilli powder 42; chillies 70, 108, 349, 350;
chimpanzees 129; China 10, 14, 25, 26, 46, 53, 62, 121, 123,
138, 146, 149, 184, 199, 299, 303, 331, 348, 349; china cups
136; Chinese 83, 330; Chios 134; chocolate 17, 102, 208, 265;
chopsticks 130; *Christ the Redeemer* 29; Christmas 31, 62, 122,
160, 172, 173; Christmas cards 161; Christmas crackers 37;
Christmas decorations 62; Christmas trees 36, 37, 62; church
121, 134; churchgoers 112; Winston Churchill 183, 243, 244;
Churchill, Canada 148; CIA 21; cigars 29; cinemas 175, 304;
cinnamon 69, 110, 140; circus animals 334; citations 142;

Citibank 342; cities 59; City of London 41; civil servants 355; civilisation 118; claret 171; Clarks 279; Jeremy Clarkson 124; classical music 80; claws 87; cleaning 228, 231; Nick Clegg 165; clerics 12; cleverness 187; climate 163; climbing 271, 287; clocks 45, 296; clothes 183, 259, 341; The Cloud 132; clouds 57, 132, 290; clover 140; clubs 202; coaches 129; coal 278; coats of arms 157; cocaine 139, 153, 256; cock 220; cockatoos 59; cockerels 220; cockfighting 321; cockroaches 74, 87, 177, 241; cocktail parties 198, 351; cocoa beans 134; codes 20, 159, 203; coffee 65, 66, 267, 274, 294; coffee berry borers 274; coffins 173; cognac 66; coinages 204; coins 31, 297, 328; coin-tossing 176, 237; cold 39, 59, 128, 135, 266, 287; Cold War 145; colds 294; collateral 201; collections 118, 243; collective nouns 87, 218, 241; cologne 102; Colombia 268; colour-blindness 103, 341; colours 163, 221, 261, 278; comets 244; communication 61, 152, 222; companies 64; companionship 128; compasses 315; competence 266; competitions 174, 325; competitive eating 259; competitors 118; complexity 295; compliance officers 342; complimenting 153; composers 113; compulsions 295; computer mice 79; computers 4, 11, 98; concrete 147; concubines 127; condoms 42, 285; confetti 69; Confucians 312; Sean Connery 278; consciousness 228; contact lenses 131; contagiousness 151, 152; container ships 190; contests 197, 321, 325; continental drift 235; continents 200; contraceptives 41; conversations 207; convicts 147; Coober Pedy 75; cookbooks 1; Mr K Cool 12; Calvin Coolidge 49; Coptic 17; coral 134, 301; Corfu 208; corn 201, 276; coronations 319; corpses 124, 162, 275, 302; cosmic dust 245; Costa Rica 85; costumes 147; counter-terrorism 239; counting 3, 26; courts 72, 95; cows 135, 159, 200, 201, 208, 276, 287, 316, 319; CPR 80; crabs 87;

cranberries 149; Crassus 74; crayon-makers 341; credit cards 11; cricket 343; crickets 343; crime 12, 38, 39, 95, 96, 256; crises 155; Croatia 22, 350; Oliver Cromwell 244; Thomas Cromwell 204; croquet 89, 325; Bing Crosby 231; crowds 116, 281; Crufts 327; cruise ships 41; crusts 173; crying 178; Cuba 319; cuckoo clocks 322; cucumbers 263; cures 100; Curly-Coated Lincoln 179; curries 318, 349, 350; cuttlefish 2, 103; cycling 39, 54, 144, 345, 345; Cyclops 148; Cyprus 22; Czech 115; Czech Republic 54, 213

DC the Demon Cat 202; Paul Dacre 231; Roald Dahl 180; Salvador Dalí 208, 296; damage-limitation 187; dance 190, 217, 320; dangers 41, 291; Danish 12, 308; dares 197; dark 303, 317; Darth Vader 56; darts 325; data 233; databases 117; daughters 135, 204; Davis Cup 193; dawn chorus 95; dawn of time 245; Doris Day 92; days 322, 308, 351; deadlines 308; deafness 138; death 44, 58, 107, 122, 138, 171, 188, 207, 270, 272, 292, 301, 320, 321, 327; debt 292; decisions 354; declarations of independence 84; deer 148, 196, 299, 314; defecating 45, 56; defence 107; degrees 305; delicacies 133; delirium 280; delivery companies 64; democracy 97, 198, 342; Denmark 69, 178, 258, 299; dentists 131, 138; deportation 168; desert tortoise 33; designers 165, 228; deterrence 107; diabetes 108; diagnoses 99, 159; diamonds 226; diaries 73; diarrhoea 190; Didcot 315; didgeridoos 52; Diet Coke 35; dieting 156; Dilbert Principle 187; diligence 53; diners 80; dinner parties 207; dinosaurs 149, 322, 347, 348; directors 217, 333; disappearance 200, 202; disciplinary committees 187; discovery 200, 300, 315, 355; discus 88; dishwashers 149; Disneyland 189; dispersal 214; displacement 257; displeasure 304; distance 3, 79, 152, 153, 214, 227, 235, 277;

distraction 263; divination 332; diving 197; dizziness 347;
DJs 286; DNA 233; doctors 99, 100, 101, 131, 156, 255; dog
lovers 128; doges 63; dogs 1, 39, 40, 188, 204, 255, 304, 318,
326, 327, 329, 332; dog-walking 40, 121; dollar bills 256, 296;
Dollond & Aitchison 303; dolphins 90, 106, 223, 240, 291;
Domino's 35; Domitian 207; donations 305; door-knocking
75; doors 270; doorways 271; HMS *Dorchester* 255; double
vision 302; double-decker buses 286; double-sided 35, 49,
176; drafts 205; dragonflies 34, 246, 247, 320; dreams 52,
325; dressing-up 321; drilling 243, 291; drinking 55, 103,
104, 129, 136, 137, 184, 338; drinking straws 211; driving 65,
123, 151, 280, 285, 286, 324; drones 34; drowning 291; drug-
dealing 153; drugs 152, 257, 268; drumming 59; drunkenness
49, 60, 73, 86, 196, 255, 258, 259, 287, 309; drying out 91;
drystone walls 135; Dubai 98; duck down 82; Dumbo
octopuses 182; dung beetles 48; Dunning–Kruger effect 187;
dustbins 182; duvets 82; dying 124; Sir James Dyson 252

Ear Phonautograph 124; earnings 161; ears 70, 124, 182,
241, 256, 260; Earth 22, 58, 70, 89, 118, 166, 167; Easter 134;
eavesdropping 332; echoes 310; Ecuador 65; Edinburgh 100;
Thomas Edison 204; editing 221, 279; Edward Edwards 217;
eels 74, 300; effigies 319; egg yolks 248; eggs 139, 164, 196,
248, 259, 261; Egypt 138, 150; eh up 251; Gustav Eiffel 193;
Eiffel Tower 193, 348; Albert Einstein 127, 259; ejection 281;
elastic 305; elderly 294; elections 16, 96, 197; electric cars
123; electricians 341; electricity 269, 278; electronic devices
313; elephant polo 238; elephants 42, 170, 171, 214, 287;
elevators 192; 'Eleven Men and a Secret' 146; George Eliot
136; Elizabeth I 319; Elizabeth II 76, 157, 196, 252, 354; elk
148; elves 30, 272; email 16; emissions 277; emojis 14, 35,

253; emus 157; energy 269; England 39, 134, 165, 217, 316; English 43, 122, 125, 180, 223, 236, 251, 330; entrepreneurs 23; epilepsy 302; equator 236; equestrianism 196; Er Wang Dong cave 46; erosion 134; eruptions 298; escapes 129, 147, 188; Pablo Escobar 268; Esperanto 224; Essex 248; estate agents 5; Estonia 22, 150; eternity 198; Ethiopia 234, 275; euphemisms 56, 299, 306; Europe 58, 153, 252; European Parliament 143; Everest 12, 287; evolution 104; exams 351; exclamations 42; excommunication 135; excrement 7, 33, 48, 100, 134, 219, 226, 253, 262, 276, 317; excreting 227, 263; execution 239; exercise 351; exhaustion 51; exoplanets 57; experts 212; explanations 295; exploding 263; exports 17, 234, 299; extinction 179, 202, 355; extinguishing 213; eye-holes 76; eyes 105, 175, 225, 247, 303

face mites 263; Facebook 30, 128; faces 51, 104, 240, 296; factories 173; fair play 240; faith healers 101; fakes 121, 145, 270, 320; falcons 55, 201; falling 159, 170, 191, 294, 321, 327; families 67, 215, 257, 268; fanfares 197; fantasies 279; farewell speeches 198; farming 23, 110, 149, 248, 275, 343, 346; farmland 252; Colin Farrell 119; farts 111, 131, 167, 206, 305, 309; fashion 279, 282; fasting 264; fat 185, 210; fathers 231; faxes 113; fears 102, 170, 198, 199; feathers 111, 226; feeding 208; fees 228; feet 10, 181, 258, 329; fencing 172; ferrets 316, 323; fertiliser 70; *Fifty Shades of Grey* 5, 6; fighting 153, 221; figs 270; Fiji 84; Filets-O-Fish 264; film critics 28; films 6, 118, 119, 146, 147, 304; filtering 94; finches 164; fine art 234, 284; fingerprints 53, 253; fingers 340; fingertips 61; Finland 17, 272, 338; fire 118, 159, 160, 193, 268, 319; firefighters 341; firing squads 239; First World War 22, 27, 122, 286; fish 2, 3, 8, 94, 95, 111, 134, 149, 195, 206, 262, 301, 317; fish food 94;

fishing 141, 207; five a day 292; flags 44, 176, 197; flames 4; flatness 316; flatworms 263; flies 219; flip-flops 348; floppy disks 98; Florida 160, 174; flowers 242; fluorescence 213; foam 13; foetuses 88; fog 46; Foggy Bottom 45; folklore 272; food tasters 319; football 4, 42, 44, 186, 193, 343, 344; football boots 237; football clubs 186; football shirts 237; footballers 4, 44, 269; footprints 171, 348; forbidden books 117; forbidden words 72, 73; foreigners 86; forgetting 227, 271; Formula One 280; Fortune 500 19; fossils 33, 226; foxes 323; France 9, 22, 54, 85, 95, 102, 125, 179, 207, 245, 252, 282; James Franco 284; freezing 185; French 6, 223, 267, 285; French air force 34; French toast 139; Frenchmen 346; fresh air 331; freshwater 89; Sigmund Freud 300; Fridays 264; fridges 25; friendliness 85, 351; friends 69, 71, 115, 128, 351; frogs 47, 347; frustration 266; FTSE 100 19; fuel 65; funerals 124, 136, 145; fungi 82; futons 86; future 98, 328, 332, 356; F-word 288

gadgets 270; gamblers 144; games 20, 143, 160; Ganges 275; gangs 256, 279; gardens 230; garlic 102; Paul Gascoigne 174; GCHQ 202, 203; geese 347; gender 103; genes 221, 292; genetic disorders 351; genitals 35, 109, 276; geniuses 335; genome 267; gentlemen's clubs 275; geographical centres 315; geologists 200; George III 232; George IV 171; German 60, 122; German army 122; German measles 111; Germany 22, 27, 39, 147, 225, 247, 284, 288; ghosts 202; giant pandas 330; giant shipworms 91; giants 279; gifts 37, 62, 160, 196; gigs 318; Gillette 343; gin 100; ginger beer 31; giraffes 171, 212; girls 142, 174, 216; Glacier Mountain Park 289; glaciers 168, 289; Glassholes 260; gloomy octopuses 106; Lucas Glover 175; gloves 175; glow-in-the-dark 75,

317; glow-worms 141; glue 81; Go 143; goals 344; goats
126, 127; goat's cheese 140; God 30, 122; Godzilla 147;
gold 199, 297; Golden Delicious 292; golden eagles 34;
Golden Gate Bridge 15; goldfish 95; golf 75, 126, 175, 241;
gonads 263; Google 117, 132, 254, 290; Google Maps 84;
gorillas 129; Gothenburg 222; gout 171; Michael Gove 170;
grammar 180; gramophones 124; Grand Central Station 193;
Grand Theft Auto 324; *The Grand Tour* 124; Grandad 301;
grandparents 306; Cary Grant 333; grass 169; grass-cutting
126; Great Fire of London 191; Great Wall of China 207;
great-granddaughters 135; Greece 100; green 247; green
beans 210; greenhouses 63; Greenland 273; greetings 251,
320; The Grimmies 174; grip 175; grocery stores 64, 179;
Bear Grylls 198; Guatemala 298; guide dogs 304; guidelines
315; guides 172; guilds 92; guilt 50; guinea pigs 188;
Guinness World Records 1, 213, 259; guitars 7; guns 298,
299; gutters 58; gyms 131

Hackney 311; hailstones 278; hair 126, 140, 260, 261, 305,
327; haircuts 183; hairdressing 305; hairstyles 140, 282;
halfway lines 236; hallucinations 104, 324; ham 210; hamsters
284; Han dynasty 312; hand luggage 288; handbags 62;
handedness 129; handkerchiefs 272; handles 243; hands 26,
109, 136, 296; hand-shaking 24; handstands 219; handwriting
205; happiness 26, 85, 340; Harambe the Gorilla 97; harbours
200; Thomas Hardy 204; harems 127; 'Hark the Herald
Angels Sing' 161; harpsichords 205; George Harrison 48;
William Henry Harrison 339; *Harry Potter and the Cursed
Child* 189; hats 110, 312; Hawaii 209; Stephen Hawking 356;
head lice 261; headaches 302; headis 193; headrest cloths
140; heads 160, 192, 193, 194, 232, 271, 302; hearts 2, 81,

140, 177, 351; hedge funds 296; hedges 189; heels 348; heirs
232; helicopters 99, 234; hello 204; Ernest Hemingway 174;
Henry VII 183; hens 98, 220, 248; Hercules 54; heritability
215; hidden rooms 192; hiding 148; hieroglyphics 58; high
five 109, 152, 340; high-heeled clogs 279; hikes 242; Ron
Hill 280; Sir Edmund Hillary 355; Hindi 156; hippos 138,
182; Alfred Hitchcock 12; Adolf Hitler 20; hmm 352; *The
Hobbit* 142; Hobnobs 265; holes 243, 260; holidays 67;
François Hollande 183; holy relics 122; home-ownership
335; homeopathy 100; hominids 268; honeybees 42; hooded
nudibranch 110; hooks 246; horizons 298; horns 74, 151,
286; horror movies 119; horses 13, 73, 144, 196, 303, 327,
343; horseshoe crabs 320; hospitals 108; hot tubs 112; hot-
air balloons 99; house prices 93; Houses of Parliament 355;
howling 332; Hubble Space Telescope 245; human race 356;
hummingbirds 81; humpback whales 133; humps 137; hunger
210, 330; hyperventilation 347; hypnotism 320; hypocrisy 267

'I Will Marry a Prostitute to Save Money' 146; 'I Will
Survive' 80; ICE 168; ice 168, 185, 186, 235; ice rinks 185;
icebergs 186; Iceland 4, 56, 85, 235, 268; Icelandic 56, 163;
identical twins 215; idiots 187; IKEA 12, 22; illustrated
cookbooks 274; Imber 286; immigration 169; imprecision
194; inaugural addresses 126; *Incubus* 224; India 8, 20, 44, 84,
96, 120, 152, 200, 234, 238, 258, 275, 278, 287, 288, 349, 350;
Indonesia 4, 44, 286; indoors 163; industrial espionage 20;
ineptitude 77; inequality 336; infestations 48, 225; infidelity
82; initiative 155; inner monologues 78; inscriptions 310;
insects 23, 159; instant noodles 26; interest payments 107;
international flights 277; International Olympic Committee
257; International Space Station 16, 43; Internet 4, 15, 307;

Inuit 76; inventions 34, 60, 98, 109, 204, 225, 250, 264, 303, 349; invisibility 225, 328; iPhones 4; IPs 254; Iran 121, 332; Ireland 55; iron 23; islands 84, 277; Israel 289; Istanbul 2, 269; Italian 69; Italians 63; Italy 5, 29, 179, 252, 261

Andrew Jackson 296; jaguars 188; jam jars 93; Jamaica 54, 279; Japan 34, 53, 110, 144, 178, 179, 201, 298, 351; Japanese 86, 163, 202, 306; *Jaws* 6; jaws 305; jeans 336; Thomas Jefferson 218; jelly 326; jellyfish 90, 206, 276; jet lag 284; jinxes 6; job applications 161; jobs 341; jogging 239; Boris Johnson 170; Lady Bird Johnson 218; Lyndon B. Johnson 35, 218; joints 212; jokes 197; Angelina Jolie 160; judo 86; jumpers 287; jumping 213, 222; Jupiter 167; juries 72

Franz Kafka 66; kakapos 152; kangaroos 33, 148, 157, 314, 326; Kansas 316; Kashmir 84; Kathmandu 315; Kazakhstan 67; keas 152; kebabs 74; keeping cool 33; Helen Keller 303; kendo 238; John F. Kennedy 120; kicking 158; Nicole Kidman 71; kidney stones 312; killer whales 95, 96, 133, 223; kindergarten 67; kindness 255; king ratsnakes 107; kings 232; King's College, Cambridge 252; Captain Kirk 224; kissing 61, 224; kitchens 208; kneecaps 353; Knights of the Garter 355; knitting 20, 287; known unknowns 169, 178, 212, 290, 300, 352; Komodo dragon 79; kookaburras 246; Kräpp 18; Kuwait 233

laces 325; ladders 189; ladybirds 164, 218; Lake Constance 277; lakes 139, 184; Lamborghini 64; *Land Tortoise* 154; lanterns 172; lap times 280; Las Vegas 165; lasers 148; last words 124; lateness 114, 117; Latin 180; Latvia 22; laughter 119, 121, 152, 306; launches 281; laundry-folding 258; lava

113; mucus 261; mulled wine 60; Mumbai 120; murder 239, 246; Andy Murray 353; muscles 194; museums 283, 284; music 80, 113, 114, 115, 231, 304, 318, 344; musical genres 10; musicals 10; mustard 160; mythology 148, 258

Vladimir Nabokov 251; nail-cutting 176; naked mole-rats 103, 130; nakedness 184, 338; names 2, 28, 43, 49, 57, 68, 73, 125, 126, 137, 162, 204, 207, 216, 218, 230, 249, 292, 300; Namibia 65; nannies 98; napkins 53; NASA 15, 16, 175, 225; national anthems 121; national debt 107, 268; national sports 83; native species 212; natural history museums 48, 222; naval charts 84; navigational cues 313; Neanderthals 101, 337; near-death experiences 141; necks 283, 346; needles 334; neighbours 13; Nepal 238; Neptune 167; nests 81, 82, 158; Netflix 118; Netherlands 115, 148, 229; neurons 330; neuroses 104; Nevada 97; New Mexico 83, 226, 255, 258; New Testament 72, 117; New Year 296, 346; New York City 10, 109, 121, 256; New York State 39, 316; New Zealand 67, 68, 188, 246, 249; newspapers 19, 118, 120, 343; NHS 8, 37, 108; Niagara Falls 291; nibbling 132; niceness 180, 256; nicknames 9, 125; Nigeria 339, 352; night 37, 75, 214, 308; nine-pin bowling 337; nipples 240; Nissan 123; Richard Nixon 49, 77, 97; Nobel Prizes 252; noise 114, 153, 317; noise-reduction equipment 149; Nokia 324; nominative determinism 12, 217, 264, 265, 285, 350; None of the above 97; normality 315; north 314; North Korea 6, 44, 49, 116, 307; North Pole 15; Northern Lights 167; Norway 13, 238, 277, 287, 321; Norwegian 12, 60; noses 51, 74, 94, 291; Nothing 289; Nova Scotia 151; novels 279; November 205; Nuba people 271; nuclear weapons 27, 49, 120; numbers 1, 332; Nutella 41; nutmeg 140; nutrition 134; nuts 41; nuzzling 74

207, 245; Paris Opera Ballet 217; parliaments 96, 334, 339;
parrotfish 33; parrots 152, 165; parties 17, 73, 128, 172, 219,
351; partridges 164; passengers 109, 149, 186; passports 13,
25; pastries 93, 190; pâté 346; patients 131, 312; pavements
115; Pawnee Farm Arlinda Chief 135; pawns 143; paws
129, 240, 328; peace sign 53; peanut butter 41; peanuts 41;
pelts 199; penguins 179, 208; penicillin 101; penises 54, 76,
159, 194; Pennsylvania 97; Pentagon 203; peregrine falcons
121; perfume 161, 162; personal space 339; Perth Zoo 71;
pessimism 140; Peter Principle 187; Peterborough Cathedral
310; petrol 193; pets 49, 74, 171, 204, 208, 297, 298, 326,
329; pharaohs 138; pheasants 170; Michael Phelps 138, 139;
Prince Philip 208; phone numbers 115; photo shoots 165;
photons 166; photos 149, 322; physics 127, 128, 260; pianos
193; pickup trucks 233, 277; pies 173; pigeons 99; pigs 105,
140, 160, 177, 178, 179, 185, 186; pillars 153; pillows 82;
Pin the Moustache on Hitler 20; piñatas 349; pineapples
232; pinhole cameras 322; Pink Lake 185; pipe organ 112;
piranhas 177; pirates 134; Brad Pitt 160; pizza 35, 36, 274;
plague 329; planets 226; plans 60, 71, 244; plants 103, 104,
230, 249, 272, 292, 293; plastic 195; plates 207; Playboy 112;
Play-Doh 102; playing cards 238; plays 205; plovers 165;
Pluto 168, 226; pockets 324; poetry 161, 204; poison 106,
194, 218, 319; *Pokémon Go* 142; Poland 22, 44, 147, 335;
polar bears 148, 227; police 12, 39, 86, 98, 151, 188, 239, 278;
Polish 36, 45; political campaigns 120; politicians 77, 96, 343;
pollen 104; Poo 289; pop music 80; popcorn 32, 311; Pope
Francis 11; popes 55, 56, 122, 319; Popeye 310; pop-ups 150;
porridge 139; portability 112, 270; Portland 176; Portuguese
349; Portuguese man-o-war 106; posh 216; possums 246;
post offices 63, 203; Post-it notes 18, 196; potholes 38;

praise 255; praying mantises 210; predators 90, 103, 106, 107, 246, 263; predictions 49, 221, 294, 332, 356; press 138, 170, 281; pressure 348; pressure pads 192; pressurised cabins 109; pretence 210, 220, 308; *Pretty Woman* 146; prey 181, 329; pride 190; priests 9; Prime Minister's Questions 119; Prince 348; printing 35; prisons 39, 122, 147; probability 23, 96, 104, 144, 151, 210, 248, 282, 283, 340; productivity 248; profit 139, 297; promotion 187, 188, 340; protection 133, 310; protein 48; prototypes 124; Prozac 265; psychopaths 331; public transport 199; Pueblo people 258; punching 256, 280; punctures 285; punishments 43; purgatory 122; purity 273; putting 175

Qatar Airways 55; qualifications 341; quarrels 77; Queen Mother 145; queues 236; quidditch 265

rabbits 265, 298, 320; race 52, 224; racing 144, 323; radiation 56; radio 113; Radio 2 248; radioactivity 213; RAF 27, 102; railways 54; rain 135, 177, 193; rainbows 163; raisins 160; randomness 104, 332; rank 188; rats 88, 99, 102, 141, 330; ravens 141; razors 343; reading 1, 156, 302, 303; recipes 140, 173, 274; recognition 271; recording devices 124; rectangles 344; red 185, 243, 247; red carpets 125; Redditch 334; Lou Reed 318; referees 187; reflection 303; rehearsals 145; reinforcement 132; relaxation 155; religion 161, 249, 338; reluctance 236; remoteness 200; Renaissance 337; renaming 216; renting 354; reports 180; reptiles 47; resources 233; restaurants 53, 80, 207, 208; retinas 166; retirement 341; retractability 240; Book of Revelation 162; reverse-flow 139; rhinos 101, 282; rhyme 309; Richard III 232; riding 327; ringing 313; rings 63; ringtones 115, 121; Rio de Janeiro

89, 188, 257; riot police 281; rivers 72, 182; roads 34, 37, 38, 65, 108; robins 323; Robocops 98; robo-gloves 175; robots 34, 78, 98, 325; rockets 134; rocks 315; *Le Roi du Crazy* 125; roller coasters 312; Rolls-Royce 123; Romania 22, 339; Romans 32; rooftops 245; rooms 270, 271; Franklin D. Roosevelt 50, 339; roosters 220; rose water 274; rosemary 227; rose-tint 275; Rottweilers 321; roulette 144; rowing 239; royal family 216; Royal Navy 84, 91, 153, 188; Royal Thai Air Force 188; royal tours 157; RSPCA 341; rubbish collectors 341; rubbish-pelting 354; rubies 57; rudeness 151; rugs 12; rules 75; running 88, 280; runways 55; rush hour 59; Mount Rushmore 192; Russia 39, 101, 144, 145, 212, 306, 342; Russian 43, 190, 308; rustling 332; Rwanda 252

Saatchi & Saatchi 38; sabrage 172; safety 285, 344; sailfish 94; St Anthony 30; St Hilda's Church 225; St Kilda 276; Antoine de Saint-Exupéry 117; saints 162; Lord Salisbury 355; Salisbury Plain 286; saliva 61; salmon 17; salt 185; samba 318; sampling 286; Samsung 64; sand 33, 209; sandals 258; Adam Sandler 118; sandwiches 139, 210; Santa Claus 31, 32; sarcasm 14; Satan 100; satellites 16; Saturn 15, 57, 167; Saudi Arabia 68; saunas 150, 272; savings 11, 201; scallops 90; scanning 294; scheduled flights 277; schools 127, 143, 180; Arnold Schwarzenegger 224; science 249, 294; scores 344; Scotland 50, 165, 184; Scots 51, 77, 155, 266; scrambling 313; screenplays 125, 224; sea 63, 184, 195, 232; sea anemones 87; sea cucumbers 263; sea level 345; sea lions 110; sea organs 350; sea otters 199; sea slugs 110; sea stars 105; sea urchin 247; seabed 63, 195, 317; seabirds 276; seahorses 320, 328; seals 227, 240; searches 254, 300; *Sgt. Pepper's Lonely Hearts Club Band* 113; seashells 106; seasickness 100; seasons 350,

351; seats 149, 297; Seattle Aquarium 222; Second World War 20, 27, 69, 93, 102, 151; secrecy 146; Secret Service 192; seeds 211, 214; self-driving cars 123, 148, 324; self-service 179; selfies 44; sell-by dates 24; sensitivity 61, 74; sentimentality 60; separate 180; September 205; Serbia 22, 190, 299; servitude 7; sewage water 17; sex 9, 10, 50, 151, 210, 212, 220, 254, 279, 320, 330; sex differences 129, 152, 215, 221; sex toys 306; sexual maturity 133; shadowgraphs 124; shadows 157; Judith Shakespeare 135; William Shakespeare 135, 205; Tupac Shakur 333; shamrocks 119; Shanghai 288; sharks 132, 133, 262; William Shatner 224; shaving 109; George Bernard Shaw 136; sheep 38, 134, 148, 179; sheep-creeps 135; Ed Sheeran 68; Shell 64; shells 64; shipping containers 40; ships 28, 40, 134; shirts 282; shoes 119, 279, 348; Shoot Me Now 97; shooting 170, 188, 298; shopping centres 116, 179; shops 180; shortages 209; shouting 309, 310; showers 35; shrikes 74; shrimp sandwiches 36; shrubs 230; Siberia 39; siblings 246; sighing 79; sight 3, 105, 247, 303, 304, 347; signs 122, 180; silent letters 216; silver 63, 196; singing 78, 95, 114, 164; singing fish 196; ski resorts 179; skin 103, 109, 111, 199; skin creams 261; skirts 282; Skittles 201; skunks 219; sky 105, 132, 245; skyscrapers 342; slang 86, 91, 309; slapping 325; slaves 92; sleep 52, 53, 96, 118, 170, 171, 295, 308, 323; slime 254; sloths 227; slowest-selling books 117; slugs 88, 230, 326; Slytherin 142; small talk 338; smartphones 16; smell 24, 32, 102, 110, 133, 162, 167, 171, 219, 227, 263, 326; Smellie 219; smelts 263; smoking 25, 212, 351; smuggling 153, 200, 297; snails 88, 230, 261, 330; snakes 100, 107; snapdragon 160; snooze buttons 52; snoring 52, 284; snow 157; Snow beer 14; *Snow White and the Seven Dwarfs* 304; snowmen 198; soap bars 323; sobering up 287;

social media 14, 253; socialising 56; socks 345; sofas 12; softness 347; software 30; soil 230; solar energy 229, 269; soldier ants 158; Somme 27; songs 113, 165, 231; sorbets 60; souls 249, 346; sounds 152, 179, 186, 236, 332; sourness 273; south 314; South Africa 179; South America 328; South Korea 39, 119, 206; South Shields 174; Southwark 354; space 43, 70, 212, 245; space programmes 234; spacecraft 57; spacesuits 15, 16; spacing 170; Spain 179; Spanish 155, 223; sparrows 82; spectacles 260, 275, 303; spectators 89, 280; speech 73, 78, 223; speech generation software 78; speech-writing 339; speed bumps 108; speed limit 34, 37, 278; spellings 127, 180, 254; spending 183, 340; sperm 220; spice 70; spiciness 318; spider silk 81; *Spider-Man* 6; spiders 6, 7, 8, 219, 342; spinach 81; Spirit of Ecstasy 123; splashing 222; Spock 224; spokesmen 217; sponge 300; sponsorship 343; spontaneity 190; spontaneous combustion 41; sport 343; spray 132; spring 301; spring onions 140; spring tides 350; sprinting 191; sprouting 211; spying 20, 21, 145; squawking 152; squid 87, 105, 220, 221, 301; squirrels 41, 78; stains 350; stairs 170; stalkers 161; stamps 31; standing 195; *Star Trek* 224; *Star Wars* 304; staring 174; stars 22; static 56; stations 228; Statue of Liberty 280; statues 54, 319; 'Stayin' Alive' 80; steak 29; stereotypes 102; sticky tape 49; Stilton 5; stoats 320; stock images 165; stocks 334; storms 162; strangers 332, 339; straw bales 137; strawberries 63; stripy tops 346; strolling 182; stubbed toes 154; students 324; studios 113; stupidity 21, 187; submarines 153, 234; subways 109, 116; Sudan 271; sugar 42, 273, 274; sugared almonds 69; suits 143; suits of armour 355; Sun 46, 166; sunburn 110; Sundays 264; sundials 270; sunshine 60, 163; supersonic jets 281; surgeons 231; surnames 219; surveillance 203;

Uranus 167; Urdu 156; urine 32, 33, 134, 182, 207, 312; US army 27, 93, 171; US colleges 324; US Constitution 120; US medical diagnosis codes 159; US PGA 175; US presidents 49, 97, 126, 182, 192, 198, 217, 218; US Secret Service 14; US State Department 45; US states 176, 316; US Treasury 50; UV light 13; Uzbekistan 150

Vakkaru Island 317; Valentine's Day 222; vampire bats 181; George Vancouver 200; Vanderbilt Tennis Club 193; vanilla 63; Vanuatu 63; Vatican City 235; vaults 120; *Veep* 119; vegetarians 24, 46; velvet 110; Venezuela 4, 93; Venice 63; venom 221; Venus 166; Vermont 75; Versailles 162; Viagra 284; Queen Victoria 156; Victorians 62, 140, 165, 309; Vietnam 28; viewers 312; vigilantes 180; Viking Squad 239; Vikings 239, 251; villages 283; vinyl 113, 123; violence 250, 256; viruses 225; vitamins 52, 177, 178; vocal cords 240; Vodafone 115; vodka 258; *Vogue* 165; voice dystonia 78; volcanoes 4, 298; Volkswagen 122; volleyball 344; Voltaire 66; volume 206, 261, 273; Volvos 148; vomiting 47, 107; vultures 107, 276

wages 19, 237, 238, 339; waistlines 280; waiting 232, 236; waiting lists 108; Waitrose 93; Wales 311; walking 88, 158, 254; Wally 181; Walmart 19; walruses 76, 306; warblers 3; warmth 114, 268, 287; warnings 164; wars 85; warships 153, 154, 234; washing 329; washing machines 258, 350; George Washington 117; Washington DC 202; Washington Monument 169; waste 296; water 89, 94, 104, 139, 166, 177, 185, 222, 229, 273, 326, 329; water skis 159; waterfalls 160, 291; watermelons 110; waving 272; We Deserve Better 97; wealth 201, 336; weapons 106; weather 17, 46, 163, 164, 266;

webs 7; websites 307; weddings 225; weekends 176; weeks 59, 227, 331; weight limits 37, 288; weights 131; Orson Welles 339; Welsh 223; Westminster Abbey 12; whales 7, 96, 111, 133, 222, 291, 322; wheat 93; *Where's Wally?* 181; whiskers 240; whisky 17; white 157; White House 35, 76, 77; white rhinos 253; Dick Whittington 356; width 209; Wi-Fi 260, 307; wig-snatching 39; Wikipedia 142; wild flowers 202, 242; William III 327; William IV 232; John Williams 304; Venus Williams 235; wills 136; willy-willies 314; Wimbledon 235, 325; wind energy 229, 250, 278; wind turbines 250; windows 75, 76; winds 167; wine 17, 80, 183, 184, 294; wings 164; winking 253; Wisconsin 254; *Wisden Cricketers' Almanack* 281; witches 75; P. G. Wodehouse 10; wolves 238, 240; women 15, 19, 110, 127, 165, 175, 197, 279, 281, 282, 305, 333, 337, 340; Women's Institute 20; Wonder Woman 97; wood 334; woodpeckers 211; Woodstock 334; woolly coats 179; working 308, 349; World Testicle Cooking Championships 299; wounds 158; wrapping paper 18; wrecks 154; wrens 164; writing 145, 156, 174, 205; Emperor Wu 127; Würzburg 27

Xmas 173

Yangtze 138; yeast 206; yellow 247, 276; Yeti 315; Yorkshire 172, 225, 251, 316; YouTube 329

Zambia 86; Frank Zappa 318; zebras 294; zeptoseconds 328; Zerão football stadium 236; Zimbabwe 127, 201; ZIP codes 203; zombie worms 96; zoos 130; Mark Zuckerberg 348; Zürich Polytechnic 127